ON QUALITY

ALSO BY ROBERT M. PIRSIG

Zen and the Art of Motorcycle Maintenance: An Inquiry into Values

Lila: An Inquiry into Morals

Robert M. Pirsig oiling the lathe in his workshop, 1975.
Photograph by Bradley Mattson.

ON QUALITY

AN INQUIRY INTO EXCELLENCE

Unpublished and Selected Writings

ROBERT M. PIRSIG

EDITED BY WENDY K. PIRSIG

PHOTOGRAPHS OF ROBERT M. PIRSIG'S TOOLS BY DAVID LINDBERG

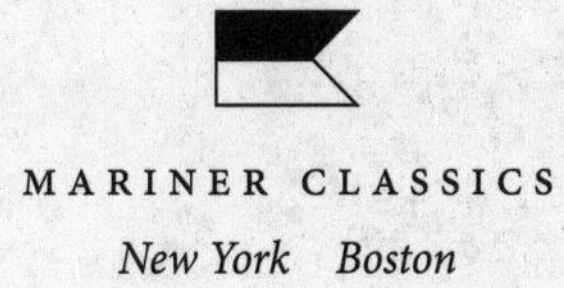

MARINER CLASSICS
New York Boston

Page 137 constitutes a continuation of this copyright page.

HarperCollins books may be purchased for educational, business, or sales promotional use. For information, please email the Special Markets Department at SPsales@harpercollins.com.

A hardcover edition of this book was published in 2022 by Mariner Books.

FIRST MARINER CLASSICS PAPERBACK EDITION PUBLISHED 2024.

Designed by Lucy Albanese
Photographs by David Lindberg
Photograph on page iv by Bradley Mattson
Photograph on page xxxii–xxxiii courtesy of the Smithsonian Institution

Library of Congress Cataloging-in-Publication Data has been applied for.

ISBN 978-0-06-308465-0

24 25 26 27 28 LBC 5 4 3 2 1

TO JIM LANDIS

CONTENTS

CONTENTS

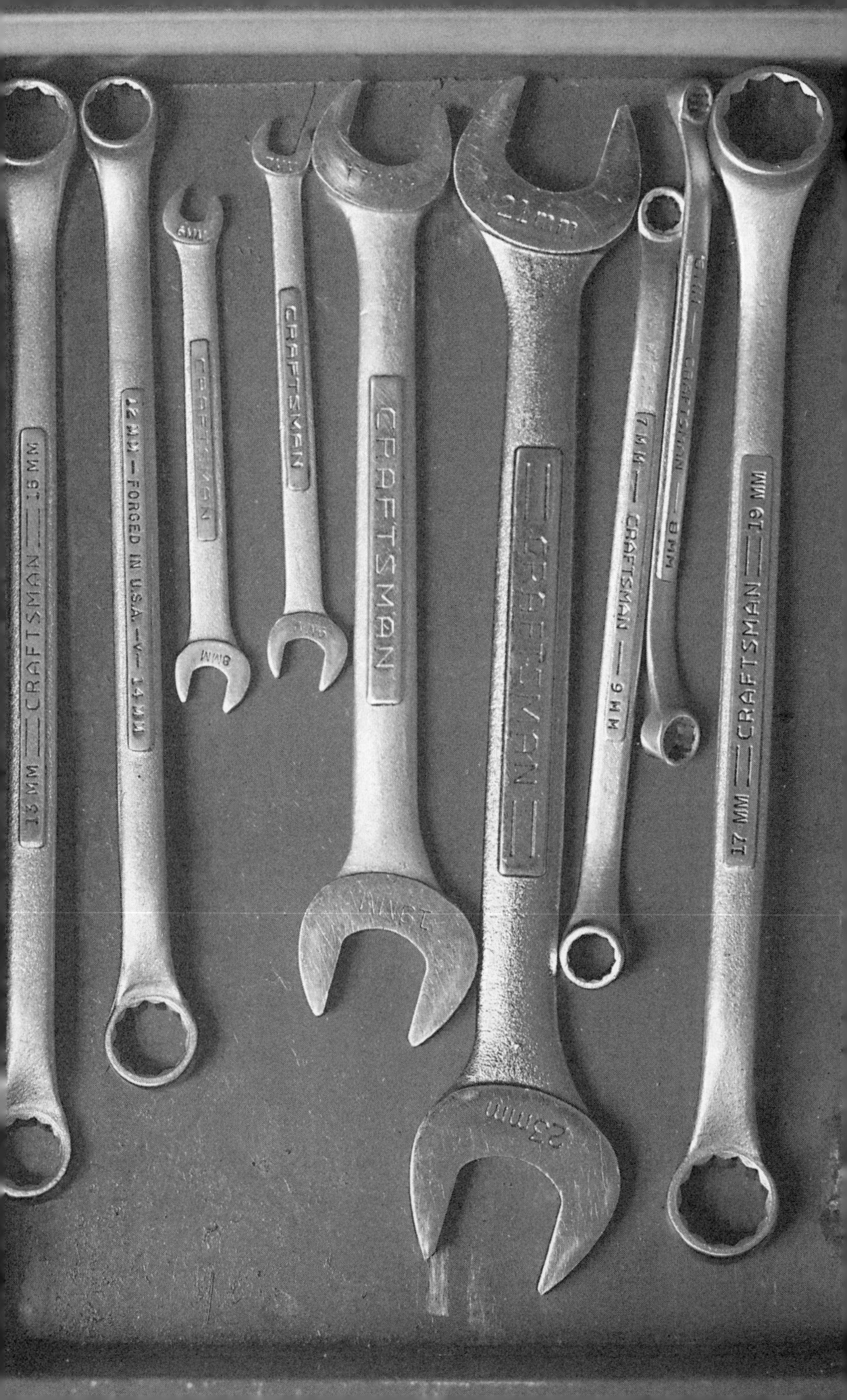

13 MM — CRAFTSMAN — 15 MM
12 MM — FORGED IN U.S.A. —V— 14 MM
CRAFTSMAN
8MM
CRAFTSMAN
CRAFTSMAN
21mm
CRAFTSMAN
23mm
7 MM — CRAFTSMAN — 9 MM
CRAFTSMAN
8 MM
17 MM — CRAFTSMAN — 19 MM

PREFACE

BOB'S QUEST

by Wendy K. Pirsig

After dark on a cold New Year's night in 1980, my husband, Robert Pirsig, and I pulled into a casino near Carson City, Nevada. We were on our way east from San Francisco, following the funeral of Bob's son Chris, who, at age twenty-three, had been murdered in a street mugging six weeks before.

The casino gave us a decent supper at a low price, and that cheered us a little. Bob recounted good memories of the days when he and his first wife, Nancy, worked as dealers at a casino in Reno back in 1954, the year they were married.

That night, with the holidays ended, the place was quiet. Bob decided to play keno, sometimes known as the Chinese lottery, the game he ran twenty-six years before. He picked up the special Chinese brush and ink and marked off the combination spelling CHRISTOPHER on a keno card, a thin sheet of square newsprint with numbers in orange squares. With gestures that still felt familiar, he made marks looking like little ship's sails.

"When I was a keno dealer, making those little marks was a way to find Quality in the job," he said.

At the window a young cashier with a pleasant round face copied our ticket with her brush. Like Bob, she made triangular blocks on the numbers. She wrote $1.00, which we'd played, and 9, the number of spots marked, with her own distinctive style. She smiled at us in a friendly way. We played to win $50,000, and lost. But we felt better than we had when we'd arrived that night.

We stood a few minutes watching the blackjack dealers before heading to our motel. They all dealt cards with smooth, trance-making motions.

"Like the keno dealer. Everybody finds their Quality operating in their job," said Bob as we left.

He often made remarks like this. Quality was on his mind.

The purpose of this book, published five years after Bob's death in 2017, is to offer a small selection of writings on the central theme of his life's work: Quality, a concept that is revealed but sometimes overshadowed in his published work by colorful descriptions of motorcycling through the American West, engine maintenance, a mental health crisis, and a father-son relationship.

QUALITY IS EVER PRESENT

At the start of *Zen and the Art of Motorcycle Maintenance*, Bob chose an epigraph he paraphrased from Plato: "And what is good, Phædrus, and what is not good—Need we ask anyone to tell us these things?" No, Bob was saying, we don't need anyone to tell us. It surrounds us, constantly guides us, and actually is us. And we know it.

"Good," "excellence," and other words for "Quality" have been exhaustively examined in philosophical thinking, especially in the scholarship of the West. Developing the Metaphysics of Quality, Bob took a new angle, placing Quality at the center of existence, where science typically places substance. Values and the ancient Greek term *aretê* are other terms he explored.

Bob's choice of the word "Quality" was suggested by chance, in about 1960, by a colleague who taught college English. Bob had been a philosophy major who had spent time in Korea in the army and then studied in India. He saw Quality as a potential unifier of two major philosophical systems around the globe. He hoped to use it in the classroom to guide students in their writing.

But he came to see that philosophical reasoning is not our only connection to Quality. Values direct our every move, every thought, every impulse, and those of all living things, all the time. And no, we don't need to ask anyone—we can see values everywhere.

Think of that: Quality is self-evident to everybody. To demonstrate, imagine a delicious food or drink in front of you right now. Feel Quality when reaching for it. Or think of music you are drawn to. The sight of someone you love. Their touch. Or imagine relief from pain. In his second book, *Lila*, Bob used the example of leaping away after burning yourself on a hot stove:

> Any person of any philosophic persuasion who sits on a hot stove will verify without any intellectual argument whatsoever that he is in an undeniably low-quality situation: that the value of his

> predicament is negative. This low quality is not just a vague, woolly-headed, crypto-religious, metaphysical abstraction. It is an experience. It is not a judgment about an experience. It is not a description of experience. The value itself is an experience.

Bob began exploring this subject when he was trying to get his students to engage their own innate sense of good writing rather than try to guess what Bob wanted as the professor. His classrooms explored various devices to reveal to the students that they did indeed recognize Quality in writing of their own and of each other. He opened up their sensitivity to value.

Bob became convinced that not only is Quality common to all living things and all experience, it pervades the entire world. The natural world, including each of us, is actually composed of it.

And yet Quality's central importance is easily missed.

Returning to the hot stove, he noted that the scientific test of burning yourself "is completely predictable." He continued in *Lila*: "It is verifiable by anyone who cares to do so. It is reproducible. Of all experience it is the least ambiguous, least mistakable there is. Later the person may generate some oaths to describe this low value, but the value will always come first, the oaths second. Without the primary low valuation, the secondary oaths will not follow."

But we don't see it as value. By the time we are cursing and jumping around, what we see is a hot stove. *Lila* argues that humans have a "culturally inherited blind spot." We know Quality, we experience it continuously, but we fail to recognize it for what it is.

Why is Quality's importance so hard to perceive? Living beings have evolved an elevated sense of "self," or subject, as a lens through which all of reality, "other" or object, is interpreted. Our honed ability to protect our individual lives creates a perception that we are separate from the rest of existence. It's all Quality, but we usually don't see it that way.

Buddhism, especially Soto Zen, which Bob studied years after he left teaching, tackles the "blind spot" through experiential training. In Zen, and in Buddhism generally, Quality/Buddha is not approached as a concept. Instead, practitioners explore such centuries-old methods as meditation, mantras, and visualizations to

bring about the realization of non-duality, nirvana, and awareness of "Buddha," "*dharma*," "*ṛta*," or many other characterizations. Concepts are actually barriers to this understanding, in which the separation of subjects and objects is dissolved. Bob's work challenges more teachers of Buddhism and other Eastern traditions to incorporate the universal experience of Quality in their teaching.

Writing *Zen and the Art of Motorcycle Maintenance*, he also knew people constantly disagree about what has Quality. That issue, and the difficulty people find in truly dissolving the subject-object split, are the subjects of *Lila*. *Lila* proposed static and Dynamic levels of Quality, and a metaphysics, as solutions.

Is it important to recognize Quality as a concept? Bob thought it was. I don't know. People don't need an intellectual understanding of Quality in order to jump away from a hot stove, or to reach for food, find a mate, or breathe. But Bob thought it is important to give Quality its due. As he wrote in *Lila*, "Things become enormously more coherent—fabulously more coherent—when you start with an assumption that Quality is the primary empirical reality of the world."

We can ask: Do academic philosophers grounded in intellectual reasoning have the ability to unify the world this way? And do most people with traditional religious understanding want to bother? Most scholars are not mystics. Most mystics are not scholars. But without understanding that subjects are not separate from objects, no one really understands Quality. And, as students of Zen and other such traditions can attest, truly grasping such understanding—without grasping and without being one who grasps!—is enormously difficult.

Bob knew this very well. Was he on a hopeless quest?

WHAT'S IN THIS BOOK

The purpose of this book is to bring readers old and new into contact with Bob's quest to develop a Quality-based worldview. Along with selected excerpts from *Zen and the Art of Motorcycle Maintenance* and *Lila*, it offers examples, never published before, of his writings elsewhere on Quality and his understanding of its meaning.

Bob's quest began in 1961 when, at age thirty-two, he was teaching college English in Montana, and his philosophical ideas solidified. There is a passage here, written years before his books, from Bob's letter to college teachers in western states about how they could encourage students to find Quality in their own work. There are some of the extensive notes he wrote in early 1962 while hospitalized for schizophrenia at Downey Veteran Administration Hospital, in Illinois, after abruptly leaving the University of Chicago.

This book includes some of Bob's writing in letters to readers, interviews (especially in the early 1990s, after *Lila* was published), and contributions to such other works as *Guidebook to Zen and the Art of Motorcycle Maintenance*, by Ronald L. DiSanto and Thomas J. Steele (1990), and *Lila's Child*, the anthology compiled by Dan Glover (2002).

Bob did not make many public appearances, but some of those rare occasions are represented here. In 1975 he gave a lecture to raise funds for the Minnesota Zen Meditation Center. He spoke at a conference of the Association for Humanistic Psychology in 1992. In 1995 he addressed a gathering of artists and scientists from around the world at the Free University of Brussels and proposed that understanding value or Quality as the basic component of the universe could allow scientists to solve a number of irreconcilable theories in modern physics.

Attentive readers might note inconsistencies here in the capitalization of the word "Quality." Bob's first writings used the lower case. When he wrote *Zen and the Art of Motorcycle Maintenance*, he began using an uppercase "Q" except in instances of the more definable, traditional uses of quality. When he wrote *Lila*, he termed the latter use *static quality*, covering "any pattern of one-sided fixed values." The term *Dynamic Quality* represented "the source of all things, the pre-intellectual cutting edge of reality." This collection of excerpts usually retains the capitalization used in the respective originals.

This book is arranged in five sections: Quality, introducing Bob's discovery of its central importance; Values, the heart of the topic from *Zen and the Art of Motorcycle Maintenance*; the Metaphysics of Quality, the philosophical system expounded in *Lila*; *Dharma*, sampling parallels to Dynamic Quality from Hinduism, Taoism, and Buddhism; and Attitude, seeking the essence of non-dualism through *metta*, a term used in Buddhism—or love, as it is known in the West. Readers may find the material in each section progressively challenging. It's worth remembering here that these are difficulties that Bob grappled with himself, difficulties that have stymied thinkers since the beginning of philosophy that can't be resolved using normal rational thinking at all.

Many photographs appearing in *On Quality* and on the book's jacket depict a selection of Bob's tools. They were photographed in 2020 by the artist David Lindberg, Bob's nephew.

THE ROBERT PIRSIG STORY

A loosely chronological presentation of Bob's life and writings is threaded through the text of *On Quality*. Although *Zen and the Art of Motorcycle Maintenance* is presented as fiction, it traces much of Bob's life up to and including an actual 1968 motorcycle trip. *Lila* is largely fictional, except for the sailboat and metaphysics, and the plot is short in duration. So perhaps a brief biography is in order, which I will attempt to summarize here.

Robert Maynard Pirsig was born in 1928 in Minneapolis to Maynard Pirsig and Harriet Sjobeck Pirsig. Maynard was a farm boy who became dean at the University of Minnesota Law School and a highly regarded law professor; Harriet was a university graduate whose early life had been marred by abuse. They raised three children. The parents' rise from their roots in early twentieth-century German and Swedish immigrant families was the context for their celebrating Bob's achievements as an early reader and chess player, despite evidence of emotional vulnerability. When he was ten, he was given an intelligence test that ranked him in the highest percentile.

Bob's admission to the University of Minnesota at age fifteen as a chemistry major ended in failure, however, and he enlisted in the army in 1946. It was one of many examples in his life of "stuckness" leading to a broadening of understanding, as he wrote later. Stepping off the train in South Korea when the troops first arrived, he saw a dusting of snow over the nearby mountains that was so beautiful and strange and reflected such a different culture that he became almost ecstatic. "I walked around. It was like Shangri La," he recalled years later. "I think I was crying. I just stared at the roofs wondering what kind of culture could have

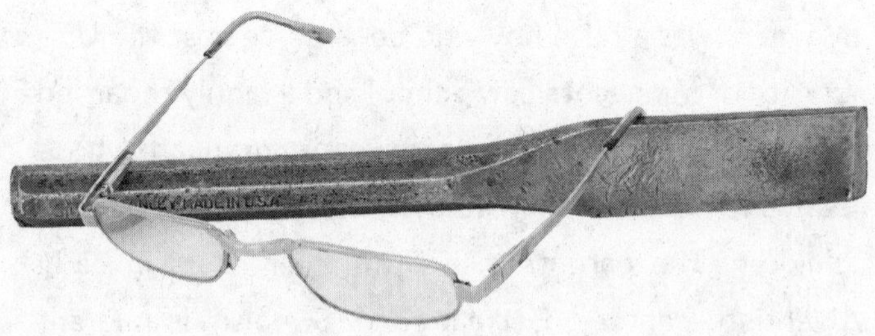

built roofs like that," he said. "That day is what started me turning toward everything in Asia."

After his discharge two years later, he completed a BA in philosophy at the University of Minnesota, then headed to India in 1950 hoping to penetrate Hindu philosophy at Banaras Hindu University. Finding the material and culture shock difficult, he started missing classes and slid into depression, suffering extreme weight loss. He was rescued by an American friend and fellow student, John Plott, an Oklahoman who had also been training in yoga. John located the owner of a water buffalo who was willing to bring his animal to Bob's house every day and provide fresh milk, which John cooked with oatmeal until Bob's spirits and weight recovered. John later attained a PhD from Banaras, became a professor of philosophy at Marshall University, and wrote a five-volume *Global History of Philosophy*. Bob's experience of impasse in India led to his openness to insights he couldn't gain in the classroom.

Back in Minnesota to complete a master's in journalism, Bob met his wife, Nancy James. In 1954 they went on the road together through the American West and to Mexico, working in a gambling casino, writing fiction, and attempting to build an oceangoing sailboat. When they returned, they had two sons, Chris and Ted.

Bob found he was more suited to technical writing than newspaper work. In 1959 he accepted a teaching position at Montana State College in Bozeman, Montana, a step potentially leading to an academic career that could mirror his father's.

But Bob wasn't suited to teaching as his father had been. Years later he recalled episodes of stage fright walking to work each morning, to the point of physical illness. But he cared deeply about academic ideals and worked not only to teach but to analyze the formal learning experience—the experience he had often struggled with as a student and now struggled with as a teacher. Why, so often, did students approach him wanting to know what *he* wanted for an assignment? What should he tell them? he wondered. And why didn't they know without being told?

It was there on campus, as he pondered these questions at the end of an afternoon in Montana Hall, that a respected senior colleague named Sarah Vinke happened by, watering plants. "I hope you are teaching Quality to your students," she remarked in a friendly way.

Quality! That was what he was trying to teach. Quality is what he wanted in their papers—the Quality they can't define but that surrounds them.

He developed classroom methods to bring this realization to his students. He began talking about it with his colleagues and experimenting with the elimination of grades. And writing about it.

But the more he thought about the importance of Quality, it wasn't just his students and educators whom Bob wanted to awaken. It was academic philosophers like those from whom he had earned a degree. And it was everyone. He wanted to upend human thinking, to bring Quality into the center of civilization's consciousness.

Leaving Montana in 1961 to begin graduate work at the University of Chicago, Bob waded into one of the most challenging academic programs in the country, and he found his ideas made little headway. Financially stressed, teaching in a Chicago community college while burdened with the demanding PhD program that "sought to define the Good in its intellectual relation to things," he again found himself paralyzed. He retreated to his family's apartment, unable to work, unable to study, eventually unable to speak. Much later he remembered little of the hospitalizations and electroshock therapy that followed in Chicago and Minnesota.

But he remembered Quality. Of course, he, like all of us, experienced Quality. But he also came away from his traumatic experience of failure, in which goals and desires were stripped away, with a realization about Quality beyond definition, beyond self and other, beyond subjects and objects. And he kept thinking about how to explain it.

Back in Minneapolis through the 1960s, Bob worked in industry. In all, his career as a freelance technical writer spanned much of twenty years. The jobs he got, for companies as diverse as hospitals, flour millers, mainframe computers, and naval defense, provided a rich background in technology. He said many times that tech writing prepared him for *Zen and the Art of Motorcycle Maintenance* in a way that was as important as owning and maintaining a motorcycle. And he, of course, did that too.

He also expanded his knowledge of Eastern religion, learning that it could produce insights of non-duality similar to those he had experienced during his Chicago breakdown. In 1957 he attended a conference on Indian philosophy in Stillwater, Minnesota, led in part by John Plott, his friend from India, and David White, a Macalester College professor who had studied with the Hindu mystic Ramana Maharshi. David's wife, Beverly White, had studied Zen in Japan under Hakuun Yasutani.

Also at the conference Bob met a former student of David White, a social worker named John Sutherland.

John and Bob began a friendship that eventually led to many motorcycle trips, including a cross-country ride in 1968 with John's wife, Sylvia, and Bob's son Chris. Another summer Bob and his younger son, Ted, took the bike on another long journey, to Churchill, Manitoba, on Hudson Bay.

Beverly White had set up a group doing Zen meditation, called *zazen*, in her home. In 1972 they invited Dainin Katagiri, who had assisted Shunryu Suzuki at San Francisco Zen Center. Minnesota Zen Meditation Center was formed with Katagiri Roshi as abbot, and Bob and Nancy Pirsig, as well as teenaged Chris and Ted, among the members. Katagiri was Bob's primary teacher about Zen.

By then Bob had taken a booklet he had started about motorcycle maintenance, which he had been attempting to fashion into a publishable work, and combined it with an account of the Montana bike trip and what he knew of Zen from the ideas he had been working with in Bozeman and Chicago long before. After being rejected by 121 publishers, *Zen and the Art of Motorcycle Maintenance* found a supportive editor, James Landis, at William Morrow and Company. Published in 1974, the book struck unexpected success, earning acclaim and readers the world over.

Bob began work on a sequel that would elaborate on Quality, centering on the question: Why do people disagree on what has Quality? Shying away from his sudden celebrity, he acquired a sailboat named *Arete* and left Minnesota, working and traveling from the Great Lakes to the Caribbean, up and down the Atlantic coast, and across the ocean to England.

In 1979 Chris was murdered while a Zen student in San Francisco. In the traumatic shadow of that personal loss, *Lila* would not be published until 1991. Nancy and Bob had divorced. He and I lived and sailed in Europe for five years, and our daughter, Nell, was born in the Netherlands.

Bob started me on a lifetime practice of *zazen*, and we eventually settled in South Berwick, Maine. We had originally met when I was a freelance journalist interviewing him for a feature story. I never wrote the article, but throughout our over forty years together I paid close attention to his thinking about Quality. Just as we did that night playing keno at the casino in Nevada, we remembered our relationship to Quality whenever we could. His goal in his books was to raise people's awareness of its central place. This is what has led me to compile this little volume.

For all the decades Bob spent writing, it never came

easily. After *Lila*, published in his sixties, he contemplated other works, but they never materialized. His work in later years involved maintenance of our home, the boat, and the motorcycle he kept for the rest of his life.

After his life's setbacks, Bob greatly relished the success his books enjoyed. As some philosophers have noted, they also challenge Western philosophy and science to take on a study of Quality and stop thinking of it as vague and unworthy. This book is meant as a reminder of that challenge.

It can be opened anywhere. Front to back, it offers some new glimpses into real events in the author's life. It is also an effort to guide the reader along a progression of ideas. I hope that any way you enjoy it, you will find Quality.

You'll know when it's there.

Robert Pirsig's 1966 Honda Super Hawk, photographed by the National Museum of American History.

INTRODUCTION

"THE RIGHT WAY"

THE LONG ROAD TO *ZEN AND THE ART OF MOTORCYCLE MAINTENANCE*

On May 20, 1974, soon after the initial publication of *Zen and the Art of Motorcycle Maintenance*, Robert M. Pirsig addressed students at the Minneapolis College of Art and Design. The following transcription of those remarks—published for the first time—has been lightly edited for clarity.

I want to talk about the creative process. My medium is books or, to put it precisely, a book. Other people work in different media. But I think my creative process is not so different from the one you may go through. And if so, then perhaps some things I say may have value to you. A lot won't. No two people are in the same situation or have the same problems. But in another sense—and this is a contradiction—everybody's in the same situation and has identical problems.

Regarding the creative process, I want to talk about two books. The first is the book I never wrote, and the second is the book I wrote. I'd like to contrast how both of those, the book and the non-book, were arrived at and, by comparing the two, try to get an idea of what was going on. And draw some morals and maybe find something useful in that process.

The first book never did get a title, and, of course, it never got written. But it was going to be a great book. My wife and I were just married. We lived in Reno, Nevada; we were dealers in a gambling casino at that time. I dealt the keno—this was at the Nevada Club—and she dealt the roulette, and we were going to save money. We lived in a cheap trailer and we saved all the cash we could. We figured the only way to beat these casinos is to work for them and take as much out of it as you can, and get out of there, and never spend a cent if you can possibly avoid it. And then go someplace where costs were very cheap, in this case Mexico, and then sit down there and write the perfect book.

So we worked for eight months. This was in 1953 or '54, and at the end we had $3,400 saved, which in the fifties was a huge sum of money, and we hitchhiked, "Bobby McGee" fashion, all the way through Nevada and into Southern California, across Arizona and down into Mexico, and then at the Mexican border got a third-class bus and went down through Mexico City, through Veracruz, way down into the jungles of Mexico and into a tiny little village town called Acayucan.

In Acayucan we got paper, and I bought a Parker 51 pen, and I prepared to write the great book. At first I found a good room, with proper temperature and proper exposure. It was nice temperatures down there, as it was fall getting into winter. Got a comfortable chair and sat down. After about fifteen minutes, after all this preparation, I said, "Well, maybe I should walk a little." I walked a little around town and met various people and talked for a while, and said, "That's very interesting, and now I'll go back and write." And I went back, and I spent maybe an hour or two hours, and really was beginning to get sort of frustrated, and not willing to admit that maybe what I had come all the way down here for wasn't going to happen.

So I procrastinated on this and other things for about a week. And at the end of a week I still hadn't written anything. I began to become gradually aware that something was very deeply wrong, that everything I'd set up, everything I'd done to come down here, wasn't right, it was a wrong situation. I was doing it badly. And then at that time an idea came along: "Well, I'll build a boat." And this struck me as one of the most brilliant ideas I'd ever had, of course, about that time, because that got me out of writing.

I tore into this boat with great tenacity. I found that you could get a trained carpenter for twelve dollars a week and you could get pure mahogany at twelve cents a board foot. We were very close to a river town, and I spent the next six months working on a boat. That never got built either, although I still have some of the lumber in my garage, and someday, maybe, I'll get back to it.

So that was the first book. It is a kind of process which I think is important to go through at one time or another. The great effort which produces nothing. The great stymie.

And now, in contrast, I'd like to talk about the second book, called *Zen and the Art of Motorcycle Maintenance*, which arrived in entirely different circumstances.

I had been a teacher of writing, although I'd never written anything, and had gotten involved with some very difficult and complex ideas about Quality, and as a result wound up in a mental hospital. After I'd come out of the mental hospital, I was ineligible for teaching work—in fact ineligible for any kind of work. I hit the streets down here in Minneapolis and started to apply for jobs one after another. The people you talk to in those circumstances are very friendly, they're very encouraging, but they know they can't do much for you, because in business they try to hire the very best people they can. Once you've got a record of mental illness on you, you're not the best person they can [hire]. They can get scared of people with that kind of background. So I was going through periods of great depression. Finally one firm by accident forgot to ask me about my medical record, and I got a job there.

That firm was Northern Pump, which became Northern Ordinance. A lot of stuff in *Zen and the Art of Motorcycle Maintenance* was learned out at Northern Pump. It's a great old firm. The tool and die makers out there, the machinists, are real artists, and if you don't know it, just get a job sometime and watch them. They're very limited in their parameters. They don't get much choice. They have to follow blueprints, but they can sure follow them well—or they can follow them poorly. They can do a piece of machinery which is very close, and they can do a piece of machinery which is right on. These options for Quality that we feel sometimes are exclusive to the arts, I feel also exist in technology. And that lesson was learned out there

in Northern Pump. It's sometimes called the world's greatest machine shop, and it really is. Entire launching systems are made by hand out there, by people in the end taking a piece of cloth with a piece of pumice on it, taking down the last millionth of an inch, very carefully.

Well, I got a job and got into that work and became a technical writer and worked very hard at this and tried to employ some of the ideas I'd had before the breakdown into the work I'd been doing. It was kind of an absorption into middle-class American life. At one time I'd sort of been fighting this and now I was trying to enter it as hard as I could, to be a useful person. I think that's important.

And I felt I did pretty well. I worked for Fabri-Tek for a while and then went to work for a firm called Century Publications, where I became a contract technical writer. This is a person who fills in when there are overloads. They used to call us the "rent-a-bodies" sometimes, or the "Kelly boys." We were the people who, when a firm had a sudden contract and not enough technical writers to fill it, would move in, get a job done very quickly, and then move out again. We got better pay and we were very free, and it was kind of a nice life, a journeyman tech writer life. This I was doing at about '66, '67, '68.

And then in the spring of '68, sitting at an office over in Control Data, writing about the Poseidon missile computers, busy, overloaded, but kind of happy about a motorcycle I had that I'd just fixed, I started to day-dream in the office. "Gee, I wish I could do a little essay on how I fixed the motorcycle and how that's not so very different from the abstract ideas of art or the religious ideas of Zen." A friend of mine, John Sutherland, owned a motorcycle and we used to go riding around in the country from time to time, and he had been talking about a book called *Zen in the Art of Archery*. And I noticed that his Harley was really firing improperly, and I thought at the time that what he really needs is not a book on Zen and the art of archery. He really needs a book on Zen and the art of motorcycle maintenance. And that was where it all started.

I want to emphasize that when that idea came, there was no preparation for it. It arrived out of my own circumstances, rather than out of a deliberate desire on my part to sit down and write. I wasn't being separate from what I was doing; this was arising out of what I was doing.

At the University of Minnesota I had a teacher named Allen Tate. He taught poetry there and was quite a famous figure. I had been in India, and I brought in a very beautiful—I thought—essay on an Indian man who used to talk to the crows while he worked. I knew enough Hindustani so I could pick up his voice and get down some of what he was saying. I thought I would write a nice story about that. When I was done, there were almost tears in my eyes, I thought it was so beautiful. So I turned it in to Allen Tate and expected great smiles of appreciation. But his answer was, "What do you want to write about all this exotic stuff for?" He said, "Write about what you know. If you write about what you know, and know personally, and know deeply, and know better than anyone else, that's going to be plenty exotic to everybody else." Anyone who has read *Zen and the Art of Motorcycle Maintenance* knows how completely that fulfills that definition. It is about what I know, but it certainly is plenty exotic to everybody else.

Now, to get back to the thread, once I'd had the original idea, I started to do this essay, which was just going to be a simple, little kind of clever tongue-in-cheek thing on Zen and the art of motorcycle maintenance. I expected it to take about two or three weeks at first. As I got into it, it became apparent to me that there are some very deep problems here. First, you can't really get from Zen to motorcycle maintenance very fast. Before you get there, you find there are underlying problems that are very deep and seem to get deeper and deeper. And so gradually, I began to discover that I was on to more than I had thought, and that this essay was turning into something quite a bit bigger.

I sat down and had to devise a way of keeping track of what were now very rapidly proliferating thoughts. Normally for a small article or a small essay, you'd use an outline, but you find that when you start getting into something big, the outline gets crossed out so fast that it becomes unusable. What I did for this particular outline was something I'd learned to do in technical writing, and that was to put down each idea on individual slips of paper and then compare them and see which went first. So my outline was always in a series of slips that went on, one after another. This is just a technique, a gimmick you might say, but it turned out, I think, to be a technique that gives *Zen and the Art of Motorcycle Maintenance* a great deal of its complexity, its fundamental sweep and wholeness, and its unification. The reviews I've read all seem to regard this as some great act of creativity. It was a very systematic, deliberate act. I was about as creative as an accountant at this point. I was just putting down these slips and comparing them. But this particular form gave me the advantage of being able to expand in the middle, of being able to reorganize at any time, so I had a flexible outline that could grow as my understanding of the story grew. I was never limited. I was free to throw away where I had been and restart again, over and over again, with what was coming in new. And I'm sure that in any creative project you really can't perceive what the end is going to be, unless it is a very small thing you're doing. I think the advantage of this particular device was that it always kept me open, it always kept me flexible, it always gave me a kind of a hollowness, so that I could constantly be refilled with new things that were coming in. The result of this was a book of many levels and of much complexity, but whose levels and whose complexity somehow always seem at the last minute to hang together.

The essay began to expand into a deep and difficult process. It became, it seemed to me, a conflict of human values and technology. That was where it was going.

Zen traditionally is seen as apart from technology, if not absolutely opposed to it, but I wished to show the relationships between the two. I began to see that what I was going to have to do was relate human values to technological values, and try to provide a uniform base by which one could get from one to the other. This got me then deeper and deeper and deeper into philosophy. I had not known that I was going to arrive at this kind of deep essay, but somehow I have a feeling there was this well of subconscious thought that was driving me toward this. The whole experience that had brought me into the hospital was now showing itself to be relevant to what I was now writing. So by leaving myself open and drawing upon subconscious forces, I was gradually seeing that my whole life was starting to come out through this little tiny essay that I had originally started.

Again, I'll repeat: not a deliberate thing where I'm coming at it from a distance saying, "Now I'm going to do this thing that was in front of me," but a kind of opening up from inside, and finding that this thing that I've started to do is bigger than I ever thought it was, and I'm going to let it grow, I'm not going to cut it off. And at that point the thing became very serious.

Of course, nobody understood what the hell I was doing about this time, and this was starting to create real problems, because I was beginning to get just a little bit obsessed. I began to feel an importance. This was starting to be a way out of past problems for me. It was going to become a new way of relating to people. So now I became very difficult to deal with. As my wife and kids will tell you, I was very uncommunicative. I would just go in my room and sit and think. I wouldn't talk to anybody. At work I would get what I could get done on the job and then devote the rest of the time to these obsessive thoughts, which were growing and growing and snowballing all the time.

Pretty soon it became apparent that I had to have time to write, that I couldn't just do it on weekends or at home at night. And so I said, "I've got to get up in the morning and do this before I go to work." So I talked to my employer, Stu Cohen, over at Century Publications, and he was kind enough to allow me to use an office that he had there. He gave me a special desk and said, "Put all your stuff in there and don't tell me what you're doing. I don't want to hear about it." It was an act of very great kindness and one that's not easily forgotten.

So I started to get up at two o'clock in the morning and go down to a little place above Robert's Shoe Store on Chicago and Lake Streets and write, mostly filling notes at first, sometimes doing sketches, and discovering my way as I went along. But writing, and then coming home for breakfast, and getting on to the job all day long, and then coming home at night and having supper, and going to bed at six o'clock: This created some terrific problems, of course. The kids were justly impatient with the idea that they should be quiet at night. It was a hardship on the whole family. Great arguments proceeded, and I finally just checked out of the house and found a ten-dollar-a-week room down on Tenth Avenue and Chicago or somewhere in a very low-priced section of town.

In other words, I was willing to say even to my own family, "Look, I'm going to do this thing, and if you block me, watch out. This is going to happen, see. This is not something that I'm really in control of. It's going to emerge now, and just do the best you can to understand." After a short time, while I hardly had any contact at all with my family, my wife began to understand that this was a very serious thing, and she made allowances. And the kids made allowances. So again it kept growing and growing and growing.

However, some of the effects were very hard, particularly on Chris, whom you may remember from the book. He was feeling very bad and very separate from all of us, and so I thought, "Well, this summer when I have a vacation, when I'm done with the work at Control Data, I'll take him on a motorcycle vacation. I'll have a chance to think about some of these ideas." So I did this, and with John and Sylvia Sutherland, we went out to Montana and over to Oregon and down to San Francisco, and from there down to Los Angeles, and then back.

At that time, the problem that was bothering me most about the writing was that, although I'm speaking out of my heart, it comes out on paper like somebody's talking from a pulpit, pontificating. I didn't know how to beat this. Whenever you write your private, personal thoughts and put them in essay form, and somebody else reads them, the vision that that person gets is that you are sort of high and mighty and talking down. I really wanted to avoid that, but I didn't know how to avoid that problem.

I didn't know what the answer was until we got to Los Angeles on the motorcycle, and there, in the middle of Hollywood, I thought, "Well, why not put the whole blessed essay in the mouth of a narrator who is on a motorcycle trip?" Then we get another dimension to the entire story. Now we no longer have a person talking from a pulpit. We have a person out in front, out in the open, in real life, a person who has errors, who

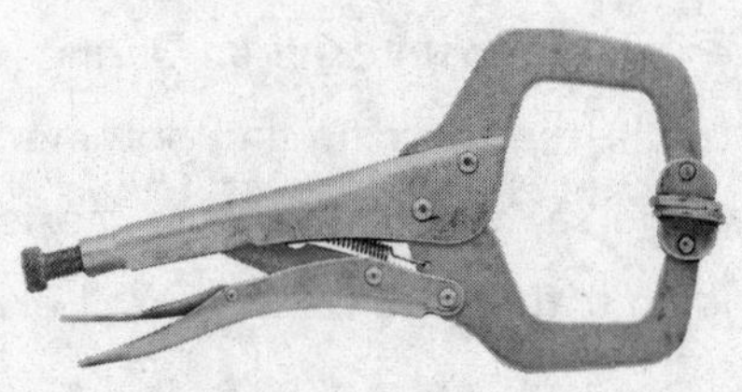

has failings, who has weaknesses, who doesn't know where he's been, who doesn't know where he's going, but who nevertheless has to try to make sense out of this as he goes. I wanted this essay to be delivered by somebody who is in the human situation. And so that became the basic format of *Zen and the Art of Motorcycle Maintenance.* At that point you can see the book as it now stands.

However, although I continued this process for two years, of getting up at two in the morning, and working until four, and had completed the entire work of 125,000 words, when I got done I was dissatisfied with it, and I set it aside for about two weeks. Then I came back and looked at it, and I was just shocked at how completely bad it was. It was just a rotten book. This is common to all the arts. I had been staring into that great crystal ball and came up with a manuscript. But now I was looking at the manuscript no longer as a creator but as a reader. And the reader, of course, has an entirely different picture than the creator does.

So I went through a great period of depression, a two-year period of hopelessness. During this time I would get up in the morning and nothing would be there. It was the same situation as in Mexico except now I was riding it through. I'd say, "Well okay, here I sit doing nothing. All right, that's how it's going to go." And then after about three or four hours of that, somehow my hand would pick itself up and start to write. And that was some of the best writing, done out of complete despair, out of a complete feeling of hopelessness about what you're doing.

Then, after the first draft was done and I'd gone through that long depressed period, I wrote a chapter. And now I knew, because of all the experiences the first time around, what this second draft was going to be like. I had the outline in my head. I was no longer writing in a crystal ball. I was writing against something that I knew and that had already been worded once, badly. And then I sat down, without any great feelings of elation or without any great feelings of depression, and hit it. Just sailed. The chapter that's now the first chapter of the book is now almost unchanged. It went from beginning to end, just completely right, after two years of failure to get it right.

I sent it around to the publishers. The night after I sent it out, a call came over the telephone: "I'll offer you five hundred dollars for it, right now, for the option to buy when you finish the book, this is it." That convinced me at that time that I better stop work at Univac and get busy on this manuscript.

So that's what I did. I took a leave of absence, and for the next two years I worked on this manuscript with great feelings of confidence that something was happening. There were a lot of family problems that continued at this time. But somehow I had the feeling I was winning all the way, that these were obstacles I could overcome. I said, at the end of the first chapter, that it was all downhill from here on. Of course, it was a two-year hill, but it *was* downhill, once that central feeling was there.

Chapters were written one by one. My wife, who had been so hostile at first, was now completely thrilled because she could see these chapters were coming up too. She is herself a writer and a very good one. She used to get very frustrated because she'd finish Chapter Two and suddenly realize there is no Chapter Three. Chapter Three is just walking around the house here doing nothing. So she'd say, "Get busy, get busy! Get on Chapter Three!" It was an entirely different feeling. We began to see that things were really going to start to happen now and get done.

Chapter after chapter came along. But one by one the publishers had been dropping off, mainly through attrition. Publishing is a high-turnover field, it's like advertising. If you're good you go up fast, but if you're bad you go down fast, and companies are very quick to exchange people who haven't been producing for them lately. So, out of the 121 publishers I had first talked to, I was reduced to about twenty-two who liked the first idea, and now down to about six by the time my second draft was done. And to these six I sent a complete manuscript of about 160,000 words. And out of this six only one finally decided that he wanted it.

I still have his letter. It's, I think, a very fine letter. There's a nice story about this person too. I've heard that articles have been written about him as a whiz kid of the publishing field. His name is James Landis of William Morrow & Co., he's kind of a wild man. I had thought of him as balding and maybe in his fifties or sixties, and I had never seen him in this entire four-year period. But about two weeks ago, my wife, Nancy, asked me to come downstairs and said, "There's somebody here who wants to see you." Now, in this wave of publicity that the book is getting, I'm getting strange people from time to time coming and wanting to see me and, you know, ask me where they should buy a motorcycle and things like this. So I figured this was another one of these folks, and sure enough it was some young guy, about twenty-eight years old, with curly hair and a beard and a neckerchief and mod clothes and just kind of a wild look in his eye. And this is my editor, James Landis, whom I've been writing to all these years. I was going to shake his hand, but I just reached up and hugged him with all my might. This one person had saved that whole book.

Well, now of course, everything has just gone bananas in New York over this thing. It's on the bestseller list. It reached number ten on the *Times* list. In San Francisco it's the number five bestseller. On the B. Dalton list here in Minneapolis, it's the number fourteen bestseller. The *Today Show* looks like they're going to put me on. I've had interviews with the *New York Times*. Next Sunday's *Times* book review section is, according to the publicity vice president at Morrow, going to come up with a book review that's the most unbelievable they've ever seen. I'm waiting to see what it is. I think it will probably be quite wild. All the reviews have been raves except a little one in *Publisher's Weekly*. But outside of that, everyone has been overwhelmingly favorable, and my life has just changed completely. That's why I'm here.

Six months ago people would wonder, "Who's he?" But now all of a sudden I'm in the process of readjusting myself—I hope very rapidly—to the new life situation I'm in. I asked for it; I can't complain. And maybe I can do something this way that I couldn't do before. I used to have a lot of wild ideas, and everybody knew it and kind of said, "There goes that guy with wild ideas." But now, because of the book, I find sometimes people listen. The ideas aren't any less wild or more wild than they were before, but I seem to be able to accomplish things that I couldn't before.

That's about what I want to say about the creative process as I have seen it and have gone through it in terms of these two books. The first one, in which I saw the book as something separate from myself, something I was going to do. I was going to be a writer, you see, I was role-playing the thing.

The second time I wasn't being a writer, I was just responding to a real need, and I was going to write that book whether I was a writer or not. This was a very important thing to learn. Let it come out of you, don't be apart from it. Sometimes I could watch my hand move. It was almost like automatic writing or spirit writing. That way of doing things is the right way, and the way that produces things of real value, where there's no separateness between the doer and the done. When that happens, you know it. You just feel it. It's just, wow. It's a whole other thing. But it takes a long frustration to reach it.

PART 1

QUALITY

One day I asked the Master: "How can the shot be loosed if 'I' do not do it?"

"'It' shoots," he replied.

"I have heard you say that several times before, so let me put it another way: How can I wait self-obliviously for the shot if 'I' am no longer there?"

"'It' waits at the highest tension."

"And who or what is this 'It'?"

"Once you have understood that, you will have no further need of me. And if I tried to give you a clue at the cost of your own experience, I should be the worst of teachers and should deserve to be sacked! So let's stop talking about it and go on practicing."

—*ZEN IN THE ART OF ARCHERY*, BY EUGEN HERRIGEL, 1948

LETTER, APRIL 2, 1961, BOZEMAN, MONTANA, WHERE PIRSIG WAS AN INSTRUCTOR AT MONTANA STATE COLLEGE

An instructor often gets the feeling that he could spend the rest of his life telling the student what he wanted and never get anywhere precisely because the student is trying to produce what the instructor wants rather than what is good.

One also notices that on many of these occasions, the particular student is as frustrated and angered as the instructor. The student keeps trying to figure out how to please the instructor, and to his way of thinking, the instructor doesn't seem to know himself. The student turns in a rambling paper. He is told he needs better organization and should make an outline. He goes to work, makes an outline, and writes a new story that follows the outline but is told the story is too dull. He goes to work, tries to brighten it with choice bits of liveliness, and brings it in. He is then told the story sounds too artificial. . . .

The solution lies in a common word that on first analysis seems as simple as the word "time" and that, on further inspection, turns out to be fully as complex as that word "time." The word is quality. When a student asks what is wanted in English composition, he should be told that what is wanted is quality.

This seems ridiculously simple at first, but it is an often overlooked and primitive concept that is absolutely necessary to put across before a student can learn to write. And it is astounding how many students arrive at the college level with no understanding that there is such a thing as quality in writing—students who honestly and conscientiously believe that good writing is a matter of pleasing different instructors, students who believe it is a matter of being flowery, being grammatical, being profound, being obedient—being anything except just plain good.

"APHORISMS," 1962, DOWNEY VETERAN ADMINISTRATION HOSPITAL, ILLINOIS, WHERE PIRSIG WAS ADMITTED AS PSYCHIATRIC PATIENT

Quality is a characteristic of thought and statement that is recognized by a non-thinking or intuitive process. Because definitions are a product of rigid reasoning, quality can never be rigidly defined. But everyone knows what it is.

Five blind men approached an elephant. One thought it was like a rope, another like a wall, another like a tree, another like a snake. All were speaking the truth. Similarly, five different people trying to describe the nature of quality may give five different answers. All may be telling the truth. There are no eternal verbal truths that tell us what does or does not have quality. The recognition of quality varies from object to object, person to person, culture to culture, and moment to moment.

There are qualities that exist in the object. . . . There is the quality that exists in the subject or the mind as excellence. But the belief that quality exists in the mind or the object is due to the basic dualistic illusion that the observer and observed are separate. At the instant quality is observed, observer and observed are not separate.

Thought of the sort used in definitions uses symbols of past experience to account for new experience. Quality is the experience before it is symbolized.

A discipline of quality is learned when one succeeds in a pure response to one's instantaneous situation uncluttered by divisive thought or past conditioning, when this response is sensitive to subtle as well as gross differences, and perhaps when one realizes that existence itself is simply this continuing response.

Of course, what one judges to have or not to have quality results largely from one's cultural conditioning. What doesn't? Of greater importance is that the growth of the culture is a response to a drive toward high or positive quality. Quality is the teleological cause of social growth.

As yet our cultural drives toward quality have been on the whole crude and primitive. The great engines of social change have not had much time to rise above simple demands for more food, clothing, and shelter, aimed at a satisfaction of the most basic desires. As these desires are satisfied by technology for huge masses of people, however, a new problem arises: What next? Our society must shift from one having developed highly complex means toward simple goals to one less focused on the means and more on the goals themselves. We will be less concerned with the national quantity of food, for example, and more concerned with the variety and quality of food produced.

The spiderlike process of analytical reasoning that is the chief characteristic of what we call civilization does not have to be abandoned permanently for an understanding and continuous appreciation of quality. Reasoning is also a part of the aesthetic universe that surrounds us. There is high-quality reasoning and low-quality reasoning. The selection of a particular line or method of reason is guided by quality choices.

The number of "facts" that can be recorded from any finite period of observation is infinite. Classes, writing about one side of a coin, have turned in thousands of "facts." It is the relative quality of the facts that causes us to choose some and discard others, for remembering.

—

Normally one's ability to see what is good marches far ahead of one's ability to produce it.

Experience does not begin with facts. It begins with monistic quality, then dualistic qualities, then pluralistic assigned symbols.

What is the difference between quality and Dewey's "experience?" "Experience" is dualistically desired. It presumes an eternal (possible) separation between source of experience and recipient of experience. A person who experiences something is separate and external to the situation he experiences, an observer. "Quality" is monistically derived. It presumes that the source and recipient of quality are not separate at all. Quality is neither apart from the world or from the self. Nor are the world and the self apart when pure quality is recognized, as they are when experience is recognized. By following a discipline of quality one eventually comes to recognize that the world and the self are not separate.

The ultimate goal in the pursuit of excellence is enlightenment. After that there are no goals, for one realizes emotionally as well as intellectually that all experience is of equal quality.

Truth is high-quality statement, quality being the determinant of reality.

The term "quality" cannot be intellectually transcended because it is both indefinable and infinitely definable (which amounts to the same thing). If it is summed up, the intellectual summary will not be superior to the term because the antithesis of the summary will be as true as the summary itself.

Quality itself is the same for everyone everywhere.

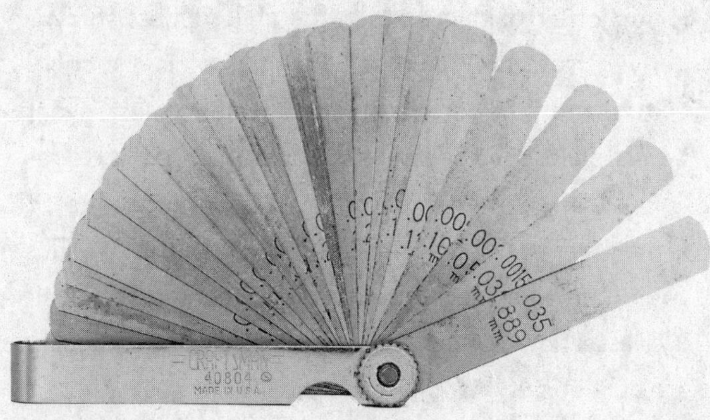

LILA: AN INQUIRY INTO MORALS, 1991

Long ago when he first explored the idea of Quality he'd reasoned that if Quality were the primordial source of all our understanding then it followed that the place to get the best view of it would be at the beginning of history when it would have been less cluttered by the present deluge of static intellectual patterns of knowledge. He'd traced Quality back into its origins in Greek philosophy and thought he'd gone as far as he could go. Then he found he was able to go back to a time *before* the Greek philosophers, to the rhetoricians.

Philosophers usually present their ideas as sprung from "nature" or sometimes from "God," but Phædrus thought neither of these was completely accurate. The logical order of things which the philosophers study is derived from the "mythos." The mythos is the social culture and the rhetoric which the culture must invent before philosophy becomes possible. Most of this old religious talk is nonsense, of course, but nonsense or not, it is the parent of our modern scientific talk. This "mythos over logos" thesis agreed with the Metaphysics of Quality's assertion that intellectual static patterns of quality are built up out of social static patterns of quality.

Digging back into ancient Greek history, to the time when this mythos-to-logos transition was taking place, Phædrus noted that the ancient rhetoricians of Greece, the Sophists, had taught what they called *aretê*, which was a synonym for Quality. Victorians had translated *aretê* as "virtue," but Victorian "virtue" connoted sexual abstinence, prissiness, and a holier-than-thou snobbery. This was a long way from what the ancient Greeks meant. The early Greek literature, particularly the poetry of Homer, showed that *aretê* had been a central and vital term.

With Homer Phædrus was certain he'd gone back as far as anyone could go, but one day he came across some information that startled him. It said that by following linguistic analysis you could go even farther back into the mythos than Homer. Ancient Greek was not an original language. It was descended from a much earlier one, now called the Proto-Indo-European language. This language has left no fragments but has been derived by scholars from similarities between such languages as Sanskrit, Greek and English which have indicated that these languages were fallouts from a common prehistoric tongue. After thousands of years of separation from Greek and English the Hindi word for "mother" is still "Ma." *Yoga* both looks like and is translated as "yoke." The reason an Indian *rajah*'s title sounds like "regent" is because both terms are fallouts from Proto-Indo-European. Today a Proto-Indo-European dictionary contains more than a thousand entries with derivations extending into more than one hundred languages.

Just for curiosity's sake Phædrus decided to see if *aretê* was in it. He looked under the "a" words and was disappointed to find it was not. Then he noted a statement that said that the Greeks were not the most faithful to the Proto-Indo-European spelling. Among other sins, the Greeks added the prefix "a" to many of the Proto-Indo-European roots. He checked this out by looking for *aretê* under "r." This time a door opened.

The Proto-Indo-European root of *aretê* was the morpheme *rt*. There, beside *aretê*, was a treasure room of other derived "rt" words: "arithmetic," "aristocrat," "art," "rhetoric," "worth," "rite," "ritual," "wright," "right (handed)" and "right (correct)." All of these words except "arithmetic" seemed to have a vague thesaurus-like similarity to Quality. Phædrus studied them carefully, letting them soak in, trying to guess what sort of concept, what sort of way of seeing the world, could give rise to such a collection.

When the morpheme appeared in *aristocrat* and

arithmetic the reference was to "firstness." *Rt* meant first. When it appeared in *art* and *wright* it seemed to mean "created" and "of beauty." "Ritual" suggested repetitive order. And the word *right* has two meanings: "right-handed" and "moral and esthetic correctness." When all these meanings were strung together a fuller picture of the *rt* morpheme emerged. *Rt* referred to the "first, created, beautiful repetitive order of moral and esthetic correctness."

Interestingly, in the sciences today arithmetic still enjoys this status.

Later Phædrus discovered that even though the Hebrews were from "across the river" and not part of the Proto-Indo-European group, they had a similar term, *arhetton*, which meant "the One" and which was considered so sacred it was not allowed to be spoken.

The right-handedness was also interesting. He had come across an anthropology book called *La Prééminence de la Main Droite*, by Robert Hertz, showing how condemnation of left-handedness as "sinister" is an almost universal anthropological characteristic. Our modern twentieth-century culture is one of the few exceptions, but even today when legal oaths are taken or military salutes are given or people shake hands or when a president is inaugurated and agrees to uphold the first created beautiful repetitive order of moral and esthetic correctness of his country, it is mandatory that he raise his right hand. When school children pledge allegiance to the flag as a symbol of this tribal beauty and moral correctness they are required to do the same thing. Prehistoric *rt* is still with us.

There was just one thing wrong with this Proto-Indo-European discovery, something Phædrus had tried to sweep under the carpet at first, but which kept creeping out again. The meanings, grouped together, suggested something different from his interpretation of *aretê*. They suggested "importance," but it was an importance that was formal and social and procedural and manufactured, almost an antonym to the Quality he was talking about. *Rt* meant "quality" all right but the quality it meant was static, not Dynamic. He had wanted it to come out the other way, but it looked as though it wasn't going to do it. Ritual. That was the last thing he wanted *aretê* to turn out to be. Bad news. It looked as though the Victorian translation of *aretê* as "virtue" might be better after all since "virtue" implies ritualistic conformity to social protocol.

It was in this gloomy mood, while he was thinking about all the interpretations of the *rt* morpheme, that yet another "find" came. He had thought that surely

this time he had reached the end of the Quality-*aretê-rt* trail. But then from the sediment of old memories his mind dredged up a word he hadn't thought about or heard of for a long time:

Ṛta. It was a Sanskrit word, and Phædrus remembered what it meant: *Ṛta* was the "cosmic order of things." Then he remembered he had read that the Sanskrit language was considered the most faithful to the Proto-Indo-European root, probably because the linguistic patterns had been so carefully preserved by the Hindu priests.

Ṛta came surrounded by a memory of bright chalky tan walls in a classroom filled with sun. At the head of the classroom, Mr. Mukerjee, a perspiring *dhoti*-clad brahmin, was drilling dozens of ancient Sanskrit words into the assembled students' heads—*advaita*, *māyā*, *avidyā*, *brahmān*, *ātman*, *prajñā*, *sāmkhya*, *viśiṣṭādvaita*, *Rg-Veda*, *upaniṣad*, *darśana*, *dhyāna*, *nyāya*—on and on. He introduced them day after day, each in turn with a little smile that promised hundreds more to come.

At Phædrus' worn wooden desk near the wall in the back of the classroom, he had sat sweaty and annoyed by buzzing flies. The heat and light and flies came and went freely through openings in a far wall which had no window-glass because in India you don't need it. His notebook was damp where his hand had rested. His pen wouldn't write on the damp spot, so he had to write around it. When he turned the page he found the damp had gotten through to the next page too.

In that heat it was agony to remember what all the words were supposed to mean—*ajīva*, *mokṣa*, *kāma*, *ahiṃsa*, *suṣupti*, *bhakti*, *saṃsāra*. They passed by his mind like clouds and disappeared. Through the openings in the wall he could see real clouds—giant monsoon clouds towering thousands of feet up—and white-humped Sindhi cows grazing below.

He thought he'd forgotten all those words years ago, but now here was *ṛta*, back again. *Ṛta*, from the oldest portion of the *Rg-Veda*, which was the oldest known writing of the Indo-Aryan language. The sun god, *Sūrya*, began his chariot ride across the heavens from the abode of *ṛta*. *Varuṇa*, the god for whom the city in which Phædrus was studying was named, was the chief support of *ṛta*.

Varuṇa was omniscient and was described as ever witnessing the truth and falsehood of men—as being "the third whenever two plot in secret." He was essentially a god of righteousness and a guardian of all that is worthy and good. The texts had said that the distinctive feature of *Varuṇa* was his unswerving adherence to high principles. Later he was overshadowed by *Indra*, who was a thunder god and destroyer of the enemies of the Indo-Aryans. But all the gods were conceived as "guardians of *ṛta*," willing the right and making sure it was carried out.

One of Phædrus' old school texts, written by M. Hiriyanna, contained a good summary: "*Ṛta*, which etymologically stands for 'course,' originally meant 'cosmic order,' the maintenance of which was the purpose of all the gods; and later it also came to mean 'right,' so that the gods were conceived as preserving the world not merely from physical disorder but also from moral chaos. The one idea is implicit in the other: and there is order in the universe because its control is in righteous hands. . . ."

The physical order of the universe is also the moral order of the universe. *Ṛta* is both. This was exactly what the Metaphysics of Quality was claiming. It was not a new idea. It was the oldest idea known to man.

This identification of *ṛta* and *aretê* was enormously valuable, Phædrus thought, because it provided a huge historical panorama in which the fundamental conflict between static and Dynamic Quality had been worked out. It answered the question of why *aretê* meant ritual. *Ṛta* also meant ritual. But unlike the Greeks, the Hindus in their many thousands of years of cultural evolution had paid enormous attention to the conflict between ritual and freedom. Their resolution of this conflict in the Buddhist and Vedantist philosophies is one of the profound achievements of the human mind.

The original meaning of *ṛta*, during what is called the *Brāhmaṇa* period of Indian history, underwent a change to extremely ritualistic static patterns more rigid and detailed than anything heard of in Western religion. As Hiriyanna wrote,

> The purpose of invoking the several gods of nature was at first mostly to gain their favor for success in life here as well as hereafter. The prayers were then naturally accompanied by simple gifts like grain and ghee. But this simple form of worship became more and more complicated and gave rise, in course of time, to elaborate sacrifices and also to a special class of professional priests who alone, it was believed, could officiate at them. There are allusions in the later hymns to rites which lasted for very long periods and at which several priests were employed by the sacrificer. [A change] came over the spirit with which offerings were made to the gods in this period. What prompted the performance of sacrifices was no longer the thought of pre-

vailing upon the gods to bestow some favor or ward off some danger; it was rather to compel or coerce them to do what the sacrificer wanted to be done. . . .

There was a profound change in the conception of sacrifice, and consequently in that of the relation between gods and men. All that came to be insisted upon was a scrupulous carrying out of every detail connected with the various rites; and the good result accruing from them, whether here or elsewhere, was believed to follow automatically from it. . . . Ritualistic punctilio thus comes to be placed on the same level as natural law and moral rectitude.

You don't have to look far in the modern world to find similar conditions, Phædrus thought.

But what made the Hindu experience so profound was that this decay of Dynamic Quality into static quality was not the end of the story. Following the period of the *Brāhmaṇas* came the *Upaniṣadic* period and the flowering of Indian philosophy. Dynamic Quality re-emerged within the static patterns of Indian thought.

"*Ṛta*," Hiriyanna had written, "almost ceased to be used in Sanskrit; but . . . under the name of *dharma*, the same idea occupies a very important place in the later Indian views of life also."

The more usual meaning of *dharma* is "religious merit which, operating in some unseen way as it is supposed, secures good to a person in the future, either here or elsewhere. Thus the performance of certain sacrifices is believed to lead the agent to heaven after the present life, and of certain others to secure for him wealth, children and the like in this very life."

But he also wrote, "It is sometimes used as a purely moral concept and stands for right or virtuous conduct which leads to some form of good as a result."

PART 2

VALUES

The quality that can be defined is not the
Absolute Quality. . . .
The names that can be given it are not
Absolute names.

It is the origin of heaven and earth.
When named it is the mother of all things. . . .
Quality is all-pervading.
And its use is inexhaustible!
Fathomless!
Like the fountainhead of all things . . .

—AFTER THE *TAO TE CHING*, BY LAO TZU, MODIFIED BY ROBERT M. PIRSIG IN *ZEN AND THE ART OF MOTORCYCLE MAINTENANCE*, 1974

LETTER, SEPTEMBER 13, 1994

Dynamic Quality is here all the time, *engulfing* both subject and object, and people become more or less sensitive to it as they become detached from existing static patterns.

ZEN AND THE ART OF MOTORCYCLE MAINTENANCE: AN INQUIRY INTO VALUES, 1974

Some things are better than others, that is, they have more quality. But when you try to say what the quality is, apart from the things that have it, it all goes poof! There's nothing to talk about. But if you can't say what Quality is, how do you know what it is, or how do you know that it even exists? If no one knows what it is, then for all practical purposes it doesn't exist at all. But for all practical purposes it really does exist. What else are the grades based on? Why else would people pay

GENERAL TAP INFORMATION
Tap Size
NC Threads
Tap Drill
NF Threads
Tap Drill

fortunes for some things and throw others in the trash pile? Obviously some things are better than others . . . but what's the "betterness"? . . . So round and round you go, spinning mental wheels and nowhere finding anyplace to get traction. What the hell is Quality? What is it? . . .

I think there is such a thing as Quality, but that as soon as you try to define it, something goes haywire. You can't do it. . . .

A few days later he worked up a definition of his own and put it on the blackboard to be copied for posterity. The definition was: "Quality is a characteristic of thought and statement that is recognized by a nonthinking process. Because definitions are a product of rigid, formal thinking, quality cannot be defined." The fact that this "definition" was actually a refusal to define did not draw comment. The students had no formal training that would have told them his statement was, in a formal sense, completely irrational. If you can't define something you have no formal rational way of knowing that it exists. Neither can you really tell anyone else what it is. There is, in fact, no formal difference between inability to define and stupidity. When I say, "Quality cannot be defined," I'm really saying formally, "I'm stupid about Quality." . . .

But then, below the definition on the blackboard, he wrote, "But even though Quality cannot be defined, you know what Quality is!" and the storm started all over again. . . .

What he meant by Quality was obvious. They obviously knew what it was too, and so they lost interest in listening. Their question now was, "All right, we know what Quality is. How do we get it?" . . .

He singled out aspects of Quality such as unity, vividness, authority, economy, sensitivity, clarity, emphasis, flow, suspense, brilliance, precision, proportion, depth and so on; kept each of these as poorly defined as Quality itself, but demonstrated them by the same class reading techniques. He showed how the aspect of Quality called unity, the hanging-togetherness of a story, could be improved with a technique called an outline. The authority of an argument could be jacked up with a technique called footnotes, which gives authoritative reference. Outlines and footnotes are standard things taught in all freshman composition classes, but now as devices for improving Quality they had a purpose. And if a student turned in a bunch of dumb references or a sloppy outline that showed he was just fulfilling an assignment by rote, he could be told that while his paper may have fulfilled the letter of the assignment it obviously didn't fulfill the goal of Quality, and was therefore worthless.

Now, in answer to that eternal student question, How do I do this? that had frustrated him to the point of resignation, he could reply, "It doesn't make a bit of difference how you do it! Just so it's good." The reluctant student might ask in class, "But how do we know what's good?" but almost before the question was out of his mouth he would realize the answer had already been supplied. Some other student would usually tell him, "You just see it." If he said, "No, I don't," he'd be told, "Yes, you do. He proved it." . . .

He had to answer the question, If you can't define it, what makes you think it exists? His answer was an old one belonging to a philosophic school that called itself realism. "A thing exists," he said, "if a world without it can't function normally. If we can show that a world without Quality functions abnormally, then we have shown that Quality exists, whether it's defined or not." He thereupon proceeded to subtract Quality from a description of the world as we know it. . . . The purely intellectual pursuits were the least affected by the subtraction of Quality. If Quality were dropped, only rationality would remain unchanged. . . . By subtracting Quality from a picture of the world as we know it, he'd revealed a magnitude of importance of this term he hadn't known was there. The world can function without it, but life would be so dull as to be hardly worth living. In fact it wouldn't be worth living. The term *worth* is a Quality term. Life would just be living without any values or purpose at all. He looked back over the distance this line of thought had taken him and decided he'd certainly proved his point. Since the world obviously doesn't function normally when Quality is subtracted, Quality exists, whether it's defined or not. . . .

If everyone knows what quality is, why is there such a disagreement about it? . . . But this argument was completely devastating. Instead of one single, uniform Quality now there appeared to be two qualities: a romantic one, just seeing, which the students had; and a classic one, overall understanding, which the teachers had. . . . And really, the Quality he was talking about wasn't classic Quality or romantic Quality. It was beyond both of them. And by God, it wasn't subjective or objective either, it was beyond both of those categories. . . . And so: he rejected the left horn. Quality is not objective, he said. It doesn't reside in the material world. Then: he rejected the right horn. Quality is not subjective, he said. It doesn't reside merely in the mind.

And finally: Phædrus, following a path that to his knowledge had never been taken before in the history of Western thought, went straight between the horns of the subjectivity-objectivity dilemma and said Quality is neither a part of mind, nor is it a part of matter. It is a third entity which is independent of the two. . . .

The world now, according to Phædrus, was composed of three things: mind, matter, and Quality. The fact that he had established no relationship between them didn't bother him at first. If the relationship between mind and matter had been fought over for centuries and wasn't yet resolved, why should he, in a matter of a few weeks, come up with something conclusive about Quality? So he let it go. He put it up on a kind of mental shelf where he put all kinds of questions he had no immediate answers for. He knew the metaphysical trinity of subject, object and Quality would sooner or later have to be interrelated. . . . Eventually he saw that Quality couldn't be independently related with either the subject or the object but could be found only in the relationship of the two with each other. It is the point at which subject and object meet.

That sounded warm.

Quality is not a thing. It is an event.

Warmer.

It is the event at which the subject becomes aware of the object.

And because without objects there can be no subject—because the objects create the subject's awareness of himself—Quality is the event at which awareness of both subjects and objects is made possible.

Hot.

Now he knew it was coming.

This means Quality is not just the result of a collision between subject and object. The very existence of subject and object themselves is deduced from the Quality event. The Quality event is the cause of the subjects and objects, which are then mistakenly presumed to be the cause of the Quality! . . .

"The sun of quality," he wrote, "does not revolve around the subjects and objects of our existence. It does not just passively illuminate them. It is not subordinate to them in any way. It has created them. They are subordinate to it! . . ."

He'd been speculating about the relationship of Quality to mind and matter and had identified Quality as the parent of mind and matter, that event which gives birth to mind and matter. This Copernican inversion of the relationship of Quality to the objective world could sound mysterious if not carefully explained, but he didn't mean it to be mysterious. He simply meant that at the cutting edge of time, before an object can be distinguished, there must be a kind of non-intellectual awareness, which he called awareness of Quality. You can't be aware that you've seen a tree until after you've seen the tree, and between the instant of vision and instant of awareness there must be a time lag. We sometimes think of that time lag as unimportant. But there's no justification for thinking that the time lag is unimportant—none *whatsoever.*

The past exists only in our memories, the future only in our plans. The present is our only reality. The tree that you are aware of intellectually, because of that small time lag, is always in the past and therefore is always unreal. *Any* intellectually conceived object is *always* in the past and therefore unreal. Reality is always the moment of vision before the intellectualization takes place. *There is no other reality.* This pre-intellectual reality is what Phædrus felt he had properly identified as Quality. Since all intellectually identifiable things must emerge from this pre-intellectual reality, Quality is the *parent*, the *source* of all subjects and objects. . . .

The Quality he was teaching was not just a part of reality, it was the whole thing. . . .

In our highly complex organic state we advanced organisms respond to our environment with an invention of many marvelous analogues. We invent earth and heavens, trees, stones and oceans, gods, music, arts, language, philosophy, engineering, civilization and science. We call these analogues reality. And they are reality. We mesmerize our children in the name of truth into knowing that they are reality. We throw anyone who does not accept these analogues into an insane asylum. But that which causes us to invent the analogues is Quality. Quality is the continuing stimulus which our environment puts upon us to create the world in which we live. All of it. Every last bit of it. . . .

He began to see that he had shifted away from his

original stand. He was no longer talking about a metaphysical trinity but an absolute monism. Quality was the source and substance of everything. . . .

Value, the leading edge of reality, is no longer an irrelevant offshoot of structure. Value is the predecessor of structure. It's the pre-intellectual awareness that gives rise to it. Our structured reality is preselected on the basis of value, and really to understand structured reality requires an understanding of the value source from which it's derived. . . .

If you want to build a factory, or fix a motorcycle, or set a nation right without getting stuck, then classical, structured, dualistic subject-object knowledge, although necessary, isn't enough. You have to have some feeling for the quality of the work. You have to have a sense of what's good. That is what carries you forward. . . .

Quality, value, creates the subjects and objects of the world. The facts do not exist until value has created them. . . .

The real cycle you're working on is a cycle called yourself. The machine that appears to be "out there" and the person that appears to be "in here" are not two separate things. They grow toward Quality or fall away from Quality together. . . .

Religion isn't invented by man. Men are invented by religion. Men invent responses to Quality, and among these responses is an understanding of what they themselves are. You know something and then the Quality stimulus hits and then you try to define the Quality stimulus, but to define it all you've got to work with is what you know. So your definition is made up of what you know. It's an analogue to what you already know. It has to be. It can't be anything else. . . .

The place to improve the world is first in one's own heart and head and hands, and then work outward from there.

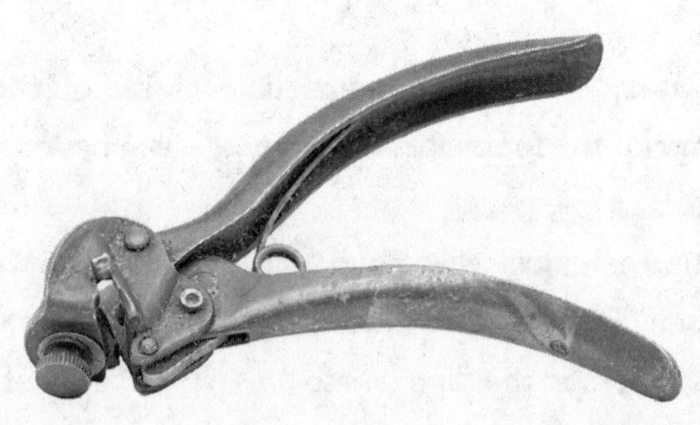

INTERVIEW, *WASHINGTON POST*, 1974

For you Quality may be Kant. For me it's hamburger. Regardless, we both want Quality.

. . . I'm trying to make the classic concepts more relevant today, helping people lead more imaginative, productive lives. The problem today is that one has to succeed in some terrible chain of values. [*Zen and the Art of Motorcycle Maintenance*] just says, "Be true to your own interests in terms of Quality." If you can go in your own basement and fix your motorcycle, that's fine.

LETTER, MARCH 22, 1992

[Quality and God] . . . are the same except Quality is never said to have whiskers or throw lightning bolts. . . . Nobody denies that there is a Quality—that is, some things are better than something else. You never have to decide whether you "believe" in Quality. How can you ignore it?

PART 3

THE METAPHYSICS OF QUALITY

Our usual understanding of life is dualistic: you and I, this and that, good and bad. But actually these discriminations are themselves the awareness of the universal existence. "You" means to be aware of the universe in the form of you, and "I" means to be aware of it in the form of I. You and I are just swinging doors. This kind of understanding is necessary. This should not even be called understanding; it is actually the true experience of life through Zen practice.

—*ZEN MIND, BEGINNER'S MIND*, BY SHUNRYU SUZUKI, 1970

“SUBJECTS, OBJECTS, DATA AND VALUES,” 1999

Zen and the Art of Motorcycle Maintenance left one enormous metaphysical problem unanswered that became the central driving reason for the expansion of the Metaphysics of Quality into a second book, called *Lila*. This problem was: If Quality is a constant, why does it seem so variable? Why do people have different opinions about it? The answer became: The quality that was referred to in *Zen and the Art of Motorcycle Maintenance* can be subdivided into Dynamic Quality and static quality. Dynamic Quality is a stream of quality events going on and on forever, always at the cutting edge of the present. But in the wake of this cutting edge are static patterns of value. These are memories, customs, and patterns of nature. The reason there is a difference between individual evaluations of quality is that although Dynamic Quality is a constant, these static patterns are different for everyone because each person has a different static pattern of life history. Both the Dynamic Quality and the static patterns influence his final judgment. That is why there is *some* uniformity among individual value judgments but not *complete* uniformity.

LETTER, NOVEMBER 8, 2005

When *[Zen and the Art of Motorcycle Maintenance]* was written there was no division between Dynamic Quality and static quality, and the term Quality then meant what is now meant by Dynamic Quality. Today I tend to think of Quality as covering both Dynamic and static quality.

LETTER, JUNE 17, 1991

[*Zen and the Art of Motorcycle Maintenance*] takes you into the mountains. *Lila* takes you out again on the other side. It explains how Quality works in the everyday world and manifests itself in ways that seem to be in conflict. . . . Why are there these moral conflicts? One key to the analysis is the concept "Dynamic" versus "static." People's Dynamic understanding of Quality, as described in the first book, is the same. It's the same for a rocket scientist as it is for a newborn baby. But all people have different static histories. The cultures they live in form a static immune system through which their Quality judgments are filtered. These Quality judgments are a blend of both Dynamic and static patterns. But because pure, unblended Dynamic Quality is not seen, except in enlightenment, the static patterns take over and the conflicts emerge.

I hope the Metaphysics of Quality presented in *Lila* can help people sort out some of these moral conflicts. A major problem of this century is that there has been no intellectual basis for making moral judgments. A lot of timidity and a lot of foolishness about making them has arisen. That has left society open to the sort of moral erosion that is distressing people everywhere these days. *Lila* offers some answers to this.

LILA: AN INQUIRY INTO MORALS, 1991

Dynamic Quality is the pre-intellectual cutting edge of reality, the source of all things, completely simple and always new. . . . Static quality . . . emerges in the wake of Dynamic Quality. It is old and complex. It always contains a component of memory. Good is conformity to an established pattern of fixed values and value objects. Justice and law are identical. Static morality is full of heroes and villains, loves and hatreds, carrots and sticks. Its values don't change by themselves. Unless they are altered by Dynamic Quality they say the same thing year after year. Sometimes they say it more loudly, sometimes more softly, but the message is always the same. . . .

Without Dynamic Quality the organism cannot grow. Without static quality the organism cannot last. Both are needed.

LETTER, SEPTEMBER 4, 1993

That line, "Without Dynamic Quality the organism cannot grow. Without static quality the organism cannot last. Both are needed," is emerging in retrospect as the most important one in *Lila.*

LILA: AN INQUIRY INTO MORALS, 1991

Although Dynamic Quality, the Quality of freedom, creates this world in which we live, these patterns of static quality, the quality of order, preserve our world. Neither static nor Dynamic Quality can survive without the other.

LILA'S CHILD (SUPPLEMENTARY MATERIAL), 2002

As stated in *Lila*, static and Dynamic Quality are in opposition to each other. Radicals and liberals who are dissatisfied with static patterns will feel less threatened by Dynamic Quality. Conservatives and reactionaries will be more threatened by it. . . .

Dynamic Quality is defined constantly by everyone. Consciousness can be described as a process of defining Dynamic Quality. But once the definitions emerge they are static patterns and no longer apply to Dynamic Quality. So one can say correctly that Dynamic Quality is both infinitely definable and undefinable because definition never exhausts it.

INTERVIEW, *NEW YORK TIMES*, OCTOBER 1991

To the extent that you perceive Dynamic Quality, you make your own life, and to the extent you cling to static quality, you are the victim of fate.

LETTER, OCTOBER 26, 1993

Quality is just experience. It is the essence of experience. That's all. It is not an intellectual category or any kind of "thing" that is independent of experience itself.

LETTER, FEBRUARY 19, 1994

Dynamic Quality is directly perceived, not deduced. It is normally thought by physicists to be subjective and therefore off limits to science.

LILA: AN INQUIRY INTO MORALS, 1991

Any person of any philosophic persuasion who sits on a hot stove will verify without any intellectual argument whatsoever that he is in an undeniably low-quality situation: that the *value* of his predicament is negative. This low quality is not just a vague, woolly-headed, crypto-religious, metaphysical abstraction. It is an *experience.* It is not a judgment about an experience. It is not a description of experience. The value itself is an experience. As such it is completely predictable. It is verifiable by anyone who cares to do so. It is reproducible. Of all experience it is the least ambiguous, least mistakable there is. Later the person may generate some oaths to describe this low value, but the value will always come first, the oaths second. Without the primary low valuation, the secondary oaths will not follow.

The reason for hammering on this so hard is that we have a culturally inherited blind spot here. Our culture teaches us to think it is the hot stove that directly causes the oaths. It teaches that the low values are a property of the person uttering the oaths.

Not so. The value is *between* the stove and the oaths.

Between the subject and the object lies the value. This value is more immediate, more directly sensed, than any "self" or any "object" to which it might be later assigned. It is more *real* than the stove. Whether the stove is the cause of the low quality or whether possibly something else is the cause is not yet absolutely certain. But that the quality is low is absolutely certain. It is the primary empirical reality from which such things as stoves and heat and oaths and self are later intellectually constructed.

. . . The reason values seem so woolly-headed to empiricists is that empiricists keep trying to assign them to subjects or objects. You can't do it. You get all mixed up because values don't belong to either group. They are a separate category all their own. What the Metaphysics of Quality would do is take this separate category, Quality, and show how it contains within itself both subjects and objects.

LETTER, AUGUST 25, 1998

Experience is pure Quality, which gives rise to the creation of intellectual patterns that in turn produce a division between subjects and objects.

LETTER, DECEMBER 19, 1995

Quality, selection, creates the world.

METAPHYSICS OF QUALITY SUMMARY (PREPARATORY NOTES FOR AN INTERVIEW), 2005

Physicists have talked about a theory of everything, but it is only about everything composed of substance. Love, for example, is not included in a physicist's theory of everything. Neither is society, or beauty, or morality.

. . . As long as substance is the basic material of reality, it has to stop when you get to things that have no scientific substance, such as love and society and beauty and morality.

But if you take the word "quality" and try to substitute it for "substance" as the central reality of the world, you get a much different explanation of things. And this explanation not only covers the everything of physics but also relates to the other "everythings" that the physicists leave out.

"SUBJECTS, OBJECTS, DATA AND VALUES," 1999

Quality cannot be independently derived from either mind or matter. But it can be derived from the relationship of mind and matter with each other. Quality occurs at the point at which subject and object meet. Quality is not a thing. It is an event. It is the event at which the subject becomes aware of the object. And because without objects there can be no subject, Quality is the event at which awareness of both subjects and objects is made possible. Quality is not just the result of a collision between subject and object. The very existence of subject and object themselves is deduced from the Quality event. The Quality event is the cause of the subjects and objects, which are then mistakenly presumed to be the cause of the Quality!

CRAFTSMAN
CRAFTSMAN

LILA: AN INQUIRY INTO MORALS, 1991

The low value that can be derived from sitting on a hot stove is obviously an experience even though it is not an object and even though it is not subjective. The low value comes first, then the subjective thoughts that include such things as stove and heat and pain come second. The value is the reality that brings the thoughts to mind.

There's a principle in physics that if a thing can't be distinguished from anything else it doesn't exist. To this the Metaphysics of Quality adds a second principle: If a thing has no value it isn't distinguished from anything else. Then, putting the two together, *a thing that has no value does not exist*. The thing has not created the value. The value has created the thing. . . .

This problem of trying to describe value in terms of substance has been the problem of a smaller container trying to contain a larger one. Value is not a subspecies of substance. Substance is a subspecies of value. When you reverse the containment process and define substance in terms of value the mystery disappears: Substance is a "stable pattern of inorganic values." The problem then disappears. The world of objects and the world of values are unified.

LETTER, MAY 17, 1993

I think Quality is the fuel that drives the struggle for survival.

LETTER, AUGUST 31, 1995

Quality is primary experience. It comes ahead of intellect and metaphysics and therefore cannot be subordinated to any system of metaphysical classification. . . .

There is obviously an evolution.

» Nothing has ever been discovered in the nature of the atom to suggest why this evolution should occur.
» No purposive teleological mechanism has been scientifically observed outside the atom to suggest why this evolution should occur.

There is obviously value in the world.

» Although there is no value in the objective universe described by science, no scientific discovery can be made without a value judgment of what is

> important and what is not. If it can be shown that "meaningfulness" is a synonym for intellectual value, then it follows that a scientific procedure that contains no intellectual value judgment is meaningless.

Since value and evolution cannot be eliminated from a description of the real world and since they are not resolvable to atomic properties, you have a real enigma on your hands. One solution to this enigma is to resolve atomic properties to value and evolution: That is, the value and the evolution must be the larger reality that contains atoms. This is a fundamental conclusion of the Metaphysics of Quality.

LILA: AN INQUIRY INTO MORALS, 1991

Why . . . should a group of simple, stable compounds of carbon, hydrogen, oxygen, and nitrogen struggle for billions of years to organize themselves into a professor of chemistry? What's the motive? . . .

Natural selection is Dynamic Quality at work. . . .

All life is a migration of static patterns of quality toward Dynamic Quality. . . .

To the extent that one's behavior is controlled by static patterns of quality it is without choice. But to the extent that one follows Dynamic Quality, which is undefinable, one's behavior is free. . . .

Not just life, but everything, is an ethical activity. It is nothing else. When inorganic patterns of reality create life the Metaphysics of Quality postulates that they've done so because it's "better" and that this definition of "betterness"—this beginning response to Dynamic Quality—is an elementary unit of ethics upon which all right and wrong can be based.

LETTER, MARCH 29, 1997

The universe is evolving from a condition of low quality (quantum forces only, no atoms, pre–big bang) toward a higher one (birds, trees, societies, and thoughts), and in a static sense (world of everyday affairs) these two are not the same.

LILA: AN INQUIRY INTO MORALS, 1991

When the person who sits on the stove first discovers his low-Quality situation, the front edge of his experience is Dynamic. He does not think, “This stove is hot,” and then make a rational decision to get off. A “dim perception of he knows not what” gets him off Dynamically. Later he generates static patterns of thought to explain the situation.

LETTER, AUGUST 9, 1995

Although it is culturally assumed that the subject-object interaction gives rise to value, a more comprehensive metaphysics is possible when one says that it is the value that gives rise to any observation. The value precedes the observation and creates the observation that, in turn, creates the thing observed. Thus value is not a property of an electron. An electron is a pattern of values.

LILA: AN INQUIRY INTO MORALS, 1991

In a subject-object metaphysics, morals and art are worlds apart, morals being concerned with the subject quality and art with object quality. But in the Metaphysics of Quality that division doesn't exist. They're the same.

LECTURE SPONSORED BY THE ASSOCIATION FOR HUMANISTIC PSYCHOLOGY CONFERENCE, JULY 1992, SAN DIEGO STATE UNIVERSITY

The purpose of each person's life is not just self-gratification. It has a much larger moral purpose, but by this is not meant some narrow-minded Victorian social restraint. A person should contribute to the quality of the world.

LETTER, SEPTEMBER 11, 1994

Quality can be equated with God, but I don't like to do so. "God," to most people, is a set of static intellectual and social patterns. Only true religious mystics can correctly equate God with Dynamic Quality. In the West, particularly around universities, these people are quite rare.

The others who go around saying "God wants this," or "God will answer your prayers," are, according to the Metaphysics of Quality, engaging in a minor form of evil. Such statements are a lower form of evolution, intellectual patterns, attempting to contain a higher one. . . .

To me "happiness" is a much narrower term than "Quality." I think of happiness as a biological response to quality in which the quality is external (objective) and the happiness is internal (subjective). Happiness is thus subordinate to a subject-object metaphysical relationship and is limited by it. All the philosophical ethics systems I have read are like this, inside a subject-object prison. When discussing the Metaphysics of Quality, the greatest difficulty you will have is keeping people accustomed to subject-object habits of thought from trying to put your statements inside this prison.

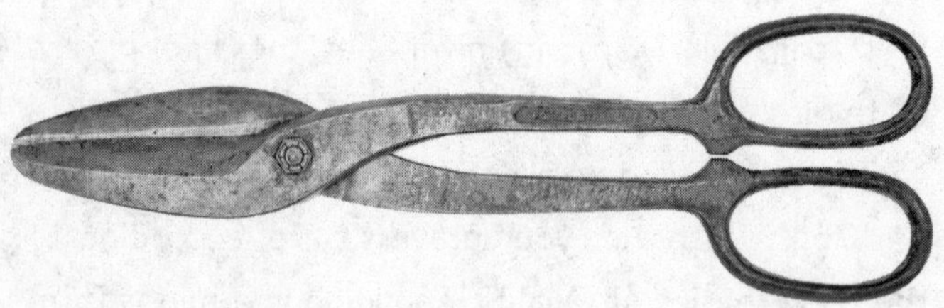

LETTER, DECEMBER 24, 1995

I used to give the students the advice, "First you just 'see' what has quality, then you figure out why. Don't reverse the process, or you will get all confused." . . .

In the West, since Aristotle, the central reality of understanding has been either the "mind of God" or else "substance." In the East the Hindus say that the central reality is "Oneness." The Buddhists say it is "Nothingness." That's quite a difference, when one considers that they both mean the same thing. At that level terms lose their meaning. "Oneness" is one intellectual path up the mountain of understanding. "Nothingness" is another such path. "Quality" is a third. When a scientifically oriented mind hears the term "substance," it says, "That's reality." When it hears about "oneness" and "nothingness," it says, "That's just empty, meaningless, metaphysical claptrap for the 'Mind of God,' which we have already rejected for empirical reasons. Scientifically those words have no meaning."

The term "quality" is superior to "oneness" and "nothingness" because it is impossible for scientists to reject it as metaphysical, religious claptrap. They try, but they cannot get away with saying there are no values in the world.

LETTER, DECEMBER 24, 1992

"Quality" is used [in *Lila*] because Sarah Vinke started the train of thought that way in Bozeman, Montana (as recorded in *Zen and the Art of Motorcycle Maintenance*). "Value" is the more customary philosophic term.

LETTER, NOVEMBER 11, 2004

As far as I know, "Quality" is still the best term, but "meaning" is a term I have thought about often. It's an excellent synonym for "quality" at the intellectual level, and I think it represents the first stage of the transition from Dynamic Quality to intellectual patterns. One first senses that some new experience is meaningful and then, because of that sense, tries to "understand" it—that is, contain it within existing intellectual or mathematical patterns. At the lower levels, however, particularly at the inorganic level, the term "meaning" is not as useful, since it is quite awkward to say that hydrogen combines with oxygen because it finds it meaningful to do so. At the biological level one does not scratch an itch because it is meaningful but rather because it is biologically valuable—that is, because it feels better.

LETTER, DECEMBER 24, 1995

The Metaphysics of Quality is valuable because it provides a central pivotal term that the Western, scientifically structured mind cannot dismiss. The second reason for the selection of Quality as a pivotal term is that it solves the "Two Worlds" problem of C. P. Snow, the division between the arts and sciences. The third is that it solves the mind-matter problem. The fourth is that it solves the science-religion problem. That atoms are static patterns of quality means that atoms can be static patterns of God without losing any of their empirical objectivity. The fifth is that it solves the esthetics problem, as shown in [*Zen and the Art of Motorcycle Maintenance*]. The sixth is that it solves the moral problem, as shown in *Lila*. There are many other problems solved by the MOQ but any of the above seems to me to justify it as a major philosophic system. That it solves all of them simultaneously makes it of unequalled magnitude.

LETTER, OCTOBER 30, 1998

Reality isn't in the mind *or* in the external world. It's in the values that create both.

LETTER, SEPTEMBER 11, 1994

All objects, whether they move or not, are physical patterns of value and are therefore static patterns of quality. Static and Dynamic are not properties of objects. Objects are a property of static quality.

Dynamic Quality is independent of all objects. It is not any kind of a pattern; not physical, not biological, not social, and (most important for you) not intellectual. . . .

Dynamic Quality is outside all patterns including philosophical rules. It is perceived directly, without intellectual mediation. . . .

This direct perception of pure Dynamic Quality without any intellectual mediation is the same as the goal of Buddhism known as "awakening" or "enlightenment."

To see more clearly why this is so, I recommend that you read Eugen Herrigel's *Zen in the Art of Archery*, from which the title of my book was taken. There, if you substitute the Zen Master's "It" for Dynamic Quality, you will learn a lot about Dynamic Quality.

LETTER, FEBRUARY 1998

Every time you discover for the first time that something is better than something else—that is where Dynamic Quality exists. There is no fixed static location for it.

PART 4

DHARMA

"As the bees, my son, make honey by collecting the juices of distant trees, and reduce the juice into one form.

"And as these juices have no discrimination, so that they might say, I am the juice of this tree or that, in the same manner, my son, all these creatures, when they have become merged in the True (either in deep sleep or in death), know not that they are merged in the True.

"Whatever these creatures are here, whether a lion, or a wolf, or a boar, or a worm, or a midge, or a gnat, or a mosquito, that they become again and again.

"Now that which is that subtle essence, in it all that exists has its self. It is the True, It is the Self, and thou, O Svetaketu, art it."

—"THE SUBTLE ESSENCE," FROM THE CHANDOGYA UPANISHAD, IN *THE WISDOM OF CHINA AND INDIA*, EDITED BY LIN YUTANG, 1942

Q & A SESSION FOLLOWING MINNEAPOLIS COLLEGE OF ART AND DESIGN LECTURE, 1974

By "Quality" I mean . . . the equivalent of the term *dharma*, which is a Buddhist term. . . . I would like to fall back upon the old philosophic statements of the Hindus and the Buddhists, who are very close on the subject of the *dharma*, only substituting the term "Quality." . . .

The ultimate Quality, the Quality that Phædrus saw in the end [of *Zen and the Art of Motorcycle Maintenance*], is a Quality that cannot be apprehended by rational means. No proofs are possible. No proofs can be given. The ultimate proof and the one that is given in the four-thousand-year-old Upanishads is "He who knows this has no further doubt." It's there, and to subject it to rational proofs is to place the proofs in a higher position than Quality itself. It's argued that this is what was done by the Socratics. They said to Gorgias, "Now you talk about the good. Please tell me about the good. Put it in rational language so that I can subject it to logical proofs." And in so doing, they elevated the dialectic, the proofs, and they subordinated "Quality," or they subordinated "the good," which is the equivalent term, or "the *dharma*," and all of a sudden we have a world in which reason dominates what's good rather than what's good dominates reason. And that I think is what I'm getting at.

So [in *Zen and the Art of Motorcycle Maintenance*] in the last, and in perhaps the most important sentence in the entire discourse on Quality, Phædrus is really done for. He's completely annihilated. And at that point, when his self is gone, when all his rational arguments are demolished, when there's nothing left, no personality, anything, then, at that moment, the Quality, which all this time he had never understood, is finally made apparent. Beyond rationality.

In the Hindu tradition there are many ways of approaching this ultimate—thing—as soon as you give it a name or call it a "thing" you are no longer at the ultimate level, but that ultimate, which is beyond the word "ultimate." One of them is the technique of meditation, which is what we practice here in Zen. Zen is, of course, a continuation of the old *dhyana* yoga, in which one just sits silently and allows one's thoughts to go away by their own dead weight. Others are *hatha* yoga, which is the physical exercise I believe; *bhakti* yoga, which is devotional; *jnana* yoga, I believe, is intellectual. All of these are ways of approaching this ultimate that has been called Quality in the book. But in each case, these are fingers pointing at the moon, rather than the moon itself. The moon itself is only apparent after the fingers have been abandoned, you see.

I can talk a lot about the wording of and the language of Quality, but ultimately the Quality, which is the pure thing—or the pure non-thing, as the Buddhists would say—is apprehended in ways that are not to be described.

ZEN AND THE ART OF MOTORCYCLE MAINTENANCE: AN INQUIRY INTO VALUES, 1974

At the moment of pure Quality perception, or not even perception, at the moment of pure Quality, there is no subject and there is no object. There is only a sense of Quality that produces a later awareness of subjects and objects. At the moment of pure Quality, subject and object are identical. This is the *tat tvam asi* truth of the Upanishads.

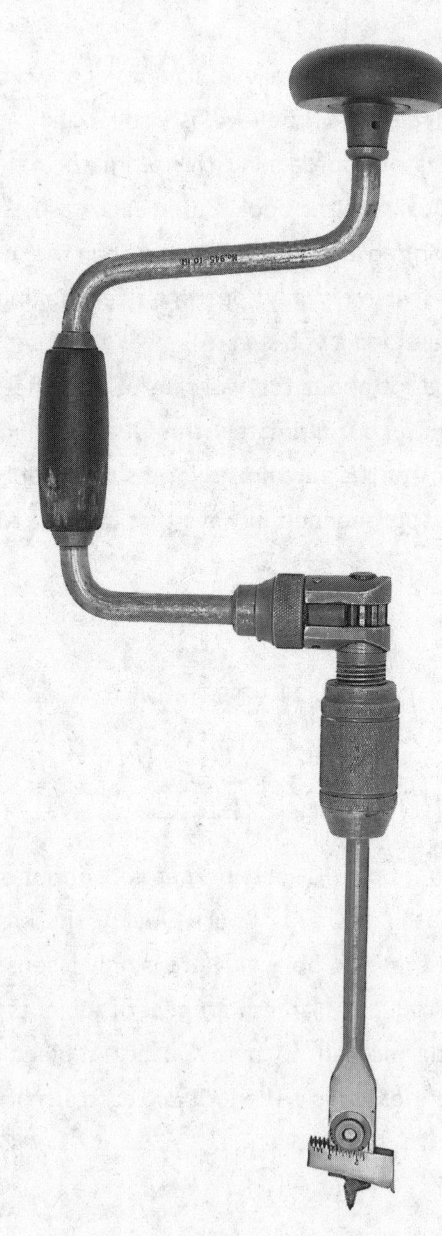
No. 945 10 IN

LILA'S CHILD (SUPPLEMENTARY MATERIAL), 2002

The best answer to the question, "What is Dynamic Quality?" is the ancient Vedic one—"Not this, not that."

INTERVIEW, 1994, UNIVERSITY OF OSLO

There is a Hindu story where the little fish asks his mother fish, "I have been anywhere and everywhere, but I cannot find this thing called water." Quality is the water that supports us all. It is the source of both subjects and objects, both mind and matter. It is everything. You may ask, "Why should we know about water since it is everything?" I say you should know it because that is the way you are learning, it is part of your evolution as a human being. By not knowing Quality in its "everything-state," you will only see a part of reality, you will be trapped in a small life. You are likely to be technically and intellectually competent without an overall understanding. The idea is to go *beyond* intellect and to *expand* reason, fully to understand the total quality of everything. When you find it, it will guide you from minute to minute, from second to second in your life. . . .

There is a link between the term "Quality" from Western philosophy and the term "*dharma*" from Buddhist philosophy. The *dharma* is of two kinds. On the one hand you have the written *dharma*, which corresponds to the static patterns of life like the laws of reason, the Ten Commandments, et cetera. I call it static quality. The unwritten *dharma*, on the other hand, goes beyond the written and is named Dynamic Quality. It is pure reality, before the intellectualization takes place. Static quality emerges from Dynamic Quality. . . .

You may see the written *dharma* as a stick with which you knock on a door. When the door opens, you throw the stick away, and from then on you follow the unwritten *dharma*. This is what Zen Buddhists in the monasteries are trying to do, discover Dynamic Quality. I once studied under a Japanese Zen master, and to know him was a remarkable experience. He lived on the edge of every second, he lived the unwritten *dharma*, where there are no rules and no guidelines. He was a Zen warrior. If you attack him, he pulls back. If you pull back, he attacks. He was flexing with the world.

LECTURE, 1974, MINNEAPOLIS COLLEGE OF ART AND DESIGN

One of the advantages of keeping Quality undefined—which is central to [*Zen and the Art of Motorcycle Maintenance*]—is that we never define it. This drives people nuts sometimes. I talk to them for hours and hours and hours about Quality, and I never say what it is, and they always expect me to say what it is. As long as you keep it undefined, then it becomes an instrument of change, and you can grow, because the things that you find Quality in are going to change as you grow.

In the past four years this book has seemed to me to have Quality. But I can tell you right now I'm getting a little tired of it. It's just past for me and now I'm looking on to something else. . . .

That's what I want, really. The intellectual structure that's been posed here is a framework in which one is free to grow and change and not to get stuck with a set of ideas that you had yesterday. I think that's really, really vital. And when you take the central term of your whole intellectual structure, and you make that wide open and changing from minute to minute and different from person to person, then you've got a dynamic philosophy rather than one that's forever confining you and forcing you into rebellion of one sort or another.

LETTER, DECEMBER 4, 1994

From an everyday world Dynamic Quality is like an undefined perfume that attaches in things, and objects are merely transitory patterns of this perfume. In the buddhas' world Dynamic Quality is the *dharma*, the only order there is.

LILA: AN INQUIRY INTO MORALS, 1991

Dharma, like *ṛta*, means "what holds together." It is the basis of all order. It equals righteousness. It is the ethical code. It is the stable condition which gives man perfect satisfaction.

Dharma is duty. It is not external duty which is arbitrarily imposed by others. It is not any artificial set of conventions which can be amended or repealed by legislation. Neither is it internal duty which is arbitrarily decided by one's own conscience. *Dharma* is beyond all questions of what is internal and what is external. *Dharma* is Quality itself, the principle of "rightness," which gives structure and purpose to the evolution of all life and to the evolving understanding of the universe which life has created.

Within the Hindu tradition *dharma* is relative and dependent on the conditions of society. It always has a social implication. It is the bond which holds society together. This is fitting to the ancient origins of the term. But within modern Buddhist thought *dharma* becomes the phenomenal world—the object of perception, thought or understanding. A chair, for example, is not composed of atoms of substance, it is composed of *dharmas*.

This statement is absolute jabberwocky to a conventional subject-object metaphysics. How can a chair be composed of individual little moral orders? But if one applies the Metaphysics of Quality and sees that a chair is an inorganic static pattern and sees that all static patterns are composed of value and that value is synonymous with morality then it all begins to make sense.

ZEN AND THE ART OF MOTORCYCLE MAINTENANCE: AN INQUIRY INTO VALUES, 1974

Phædrus is fascinated too by the description of the motive of "duty toward self" which is an almost exact translation of the Sanskrit word *dharma*, sometimes described as the "one" of the Hindus. Can the *dharma* of the Hindus and the "virtue" of the ancient Greeks be identical?

LETTER, JULY 30, 1996

Dynamic Quality is described as unwritten *dharma*. Before enlightenment one should follow the written *dharma*—that is, static patterns of morality as they have been set down in the past by the enlightened ones—and use them for moral guidance. Dynamic Quality can be trusted completely only after enlightenment.

LETTER, NOVEMBER 25, 1992

So far [readers seem] struck mute about the equivalence of the terms "Quality" and "*dharma*," which are both derived from a common prehistoric root, "*ṛta*," meaning "the cosmic order of things." The Buddhists have no trouble understanding that the *dharma* is the origin of things, but I think it's going to take another century or two to convince Westerners that Quality is. . . . Eventually I think this dharma=Quality equivalence can open up a floodgate of Oriental understanding upon the meaning of "values" in this country. . . . There is so much to learn about *dharma* from Asia.

LETTER, FEBRUARY 5, 1994

Everyone has a personal *dharma*, which could be defined as "duty to Quality."

INTERVIEW, *OUI*, NOVEMBER 1975

The drive for Quality is a natural drive. Everybody wants to do things better; everybody wants to have things better. Nobody wants anything worse than it was before. . . .

I can't put Quality into an exact intellectual framework for you any more than the Zen Buddhists can put the *dharma* that they speak of into an absolute framework. Whatever framework you choose is always less than the *dharma* itself, and whatever definition you give of Quality is always less than Quality itself.

LETTER, FEBRUARY 23, 1992

Dynamic Quality isn't unseeable or untouchable. Dynamic Quality is wall-to-wall sensory experience. But the distinctions of seeing and touching are not made.

LILA: AN INQUIRY INTO MORALS, 1991

There's a famous [Zen] poem that goes:

While living,
Be a dead man.
Be completely dead,
And then do as you please.
And all will be well.

It sounds like something from a Hollywood horror-film but it's about nirvana. The Metaphysics of Quality translates it:

While sustaining biological and social patterns
Kill all intellectual patterns.
Kill them completely
And then follow Dynamic Quality
And morality will be served.

LETTER, APRIL 24, 1992

Quality and spirituality are synonymous, so that a metaphysics of quality is in fact a metaphysics of spirituality. There is Dynamic spirituality, which is undefinable; and static spirituality, which consists of intellectual spirituality (theology), social spirituality (church), and biological spirituality (ritual).

LETTER, APRIL 28, 1997

When explaining Quality becomes difficult, it can mean that you are subordinating Dynamic Quality to the rules of static dialectical reasoning. It means you are accepting the dialectician's belief that if a thing can't be handled dialectically it isn't real and trying to make Quality conform to this reality. But learning what Quality really is requires not an addition of dialectical knowledge but a subtraction of dialectical knowledge to see the Quality that is always present. That is what the Zen meditation is for—to subtract knowledge.

ZEN AND THE ART OF MOTORCYCLE MAINTENANCE: AN INQUIRY INTO VALUES, 1974

Because we're unaccustomed to it, we don't usually see that there's a third possible logical term equal to yes and no which is capable of expanding our understanding in an unrecognized direction. We don't even have a term for it, so I'll have to use the Japanese *mu*. *Mu* means "no thing." Like "Quality" it points outside the process of dualistic discrimination. *Mu* simply says, "No class; not one, not zero, not yes, not no." It states that the context of the question is such that a yes or no answer is in error and should not be given. "Unask the question" is what it says. *Mu* becomes appropriate when the context of the question becomes too small for the truth of the answer. When the Zen monk Joshu was asked whether a dog had a Buddha-nature he said "*Mu*," meaning that if he answered either way he was answering incorrectly. The Buddha-nature cannot be captured by yes or no questions.

LETTER, APRIL 30, 1997

The fundamental formula for the relation of the Metaphysics of Quality to Zen is: "Quality equals Buddha-nature." So if you want to know what Quality is, you can find the answer by learning what Buddha-nature is.

LETTER, DECEMBER 9, 1992

Between the Tao and the unwritten *dharma* and Quality I see no difference at all, and this equivalence can be a kind of Rosetta Stone for translating the meaning of some otherwise inscrutable Oriental texts into scientific language.

LETTER, JANUARY 25, 1992

I have a Japanese calligraphic painting . . . on my wall that says, "In nothingness there is a great working." This calligraphy was made for my son Chris by his late teacher, Dainin Katagiri Roshi, and expresses a most profound concept of Zen. This "nothingness" is also what I mean by Dynamic Quality.

LETTER, FEBRUARY 12, 1997

Dynamic Quality is not the result of any symmetries or patterns but is rather the source of patterns and symmetries and is inherent in them. It is what the Buddhist understands when he refers to "nirvana" or "nothingness," and says, "Within nothingness there is a great working."

LETTER, OCTOBER 7, 2004

The Quality that is everything that exists is Dynamic Quality. It includes within it static quality, which is full of distinctions, including distinctions between good and bad. All this, as far as I know, agrees with standard Buddhist doctrine. . . .

The characterization of the Buddha's world as "nothingness" has been a source of Western confusion, leading some to consider Buddhist nirvana as a form of suicide. What is meant by Buddhist "nothingness" is "no thingness"—that is, "no objectivity." Since the use of the undefined term "Quality" denies objectivity without suggesting that nirvana is some kind of vacuum, it helps to clarify what Buddhist nothingness is.

LETTER, SEPTEMBER (UNDATED) 1992

The question isn't, "Is Quality real?" That has already been answered. You can't live without it. The question is, "Why can't we define it?" . . . We can't define it because our defining apparatus (subject-object metaphysics) is inadequate.

The best way of investigating Quality that I know of is the brilliant Oriental technique of *zazen*, which defines Dynamic Quality very precisely by forcing a subtraction of static intellectual patterns for it rather than adding new ones.

LETTER, SEPTEMBER 27, 1994

So the only question is how to achieve real Quality, and for that I would recommend Zen meditation. Find a Zen group in your area and attend. Then if you discover the real Quality, the real *dharma* of your life . . . you will be doing the right thing.

LETTER, AUGUST 17, 1997

Everybody knows what Quality is. Some people know that they know it, and other people, particularly freshman rhetoric students, don't know that they know it. This is in accord with the Soto Zen Buddhist doctrine that everyone is enlightened. What occurs at "enlightenment" is the falling away of the illusion that one is not enlightened. But the enlightenment has been there all along.

LETTER, SEPTEMBER 23, 1993

Dynamic Quality, in its pure form, is the equivalent of Buddhist *nirvana*.

Q & A SESSION, 1974, MINNEAPOLIS COLLEGE OF ART AND DESIGN

The important thing is not to be contained by intellect but to simply use it as an instrument. When we were all sitting over at Beverly White's house in St. Paul, as Zen Buddhists, we used to from time to time put up a *koan*, or some statement that was very difficult—they weren't really *koans*—and after about half an hour we'd all give our comment on what it meant. And one of the *koans* that came up was, "Of what use are words?" And then we all sat for half an hour. And, of course, when [it was] time to answer almost nobody answered, which is a nice Zen answer. Except me, being a writer and an intellectual, felt a little bit on the spot. So I said, "Well, words like 'hands' and 'feet' are not necessary, but they're plenty useful." And I think that the ultimate understanding of Quality is wordless, but that the Quality inheres in the words you use. Throughout [*Zen and the Art of Motorcycle Maintenance*] I have felt the very strong mandate to be very sure that I was saying these things in a high-quality way, and not getting into the philosopher's trap of talking about beauty in the most ugly language possible.

I think that our traditional Western way is to try to capture life in a net of words. But I think one can realize that the net of words *is* a part of life. The danger is not in using the words; the danger is in clinging to them, clinging to their meaning, and saying, "Oh, now I have spoken a great truth."

There is a wonderful line by Shunryu Suzuki, who died recently, in his book *Zen Mind, Beginner's Mind*, which I feel is one of the best ever written, in which he says [in effect], "When I'm all done with this lecture you should forget every word I've said."* And you think, "Well now, what are we sitting here for, if this is the case?" But this is one of the most profound statements he could have made. He was using words but he didn't want you to cling to them. He simply wanted you to absorb them and make them a part of you, and carry on the *dharma*, and words could be a useful instrument for this purpose.

So the philosophy, the analysis, the bright monkeyshines that are going on in the philosophic realm in [*Zen and the Art of Motorcycle Maintenance*] are instruments. And again the vital line is that in the end Phædrus never understood what Quality was, all the time he had derived all these huge, vast, intellectual matrices for it.

* *Zen Mind, Beginner's Mind*, by Shunryu Suzuki (1970): "There is no need to remember what I say."

PART 5

ATTITUDE

May all beings be at ease!

Let none deceive another,
Or despise any being in any state.
Let none through anger or ill-will
Wish harm upon another.
Even as a mother protects with her life
Her child, her only child,
So with a boundless heart
Should one cherish all living beings;
Radiating kindness over the entire world:
Spreading upwards to the skies,
And downwards to the depths;
Outwards and unbounded,

Freed from hatred and ill-will.

Whether standing or walking, seated

or lying down

Free from drowsiness,

One should sustain this recollection.

This is said to be the sublime abiding.

—*KARANIYA METTA SUTTA: THE BUDDHA'S WORDS ON LOVING-KINDNESS*, TRANSLATED FROM THE PALI BY THE AMARAVATI SANGHA, 2004

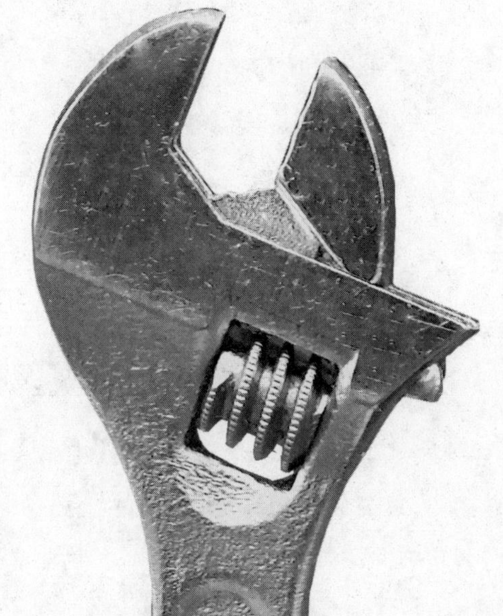
150mm FORGED IN USA
44602

ZEN AND THE ART OF MOTORCYCLE MAINTENANCE: AN INQUIRY INTO VALUES, 1974

As we ride now through coastal manzanita and waxen-leafed shrubs, Chris's expression comes to mind. "I knew it," he said.

The cycle swings into each curve effortlessly, banking so that our weight is always down through the machine no matter what its angle is with the ground. The way is full of flowers and surprise views, tight turns one after another so that the whole world rolls and pirouettes and rises and falls away.

"I knew it," he said. It comes back now as one of those little facts tugging at the end of a line, saying it's not as small as I think it is. It's been in his mind for a long time. Years. All the problems he's given become more understandable. "I *knew* it," he said.

He must have heard something long ago, and in his childish misunderstanding gotten it all mixed up. That's what Phædrus always said—I always said—years ago, and Chris must have believed it, and kept it hidden inside ever since.

We're related to each other in ways we never fully understand, maybe hardly understand at all. He was always the real reason for coming out of the hospital. To have let him grow up alone would have been really wrong. In the dream too he was the one who was always trying to open the door.

I haven't been carrying him at all. He's been carrying *me*! "I *knew* it," he said. It keeps tugging on the line, saying my big problem may not be as big as I think it is, because the answer is right in front of me. For God's sake relieve him of his burden! Be one person again!

Rich air and strange perfumes from the flowers of the trees and shrubs enshroud us. Inland now the chill is gone and the heat is upon us again. It soaks through my jacket and clothes and dries out the dampness inside. The gloves which have been dark-wet have started to turn light again. It seems like I've been bone-chilled by that ocean damp for so long I've forgotten what heat is like. I begin to feel drowsy and in a small ravine ahead I see a turnoff and a picnic table. When we get to it I cut the engine and stop.

"I'm sleepy," I tell Chris. "I'm going to take a nap."

"Me too," he says.

We sleep and when we wake up I feel very rested, more rested than for a long time. I take Chris's jacket and mine and tuck them under the elastic cables holding down the pack on the cycle.

It's so hot I feel like leaving this helmet off. I remember that in this state they're not required. I fasten it around one of the cables.

"Put mine there too," Chris says.

"You need it for safety."

"You're not wearing yours."

"All right," I agree, and stow his too.

The road continues to twist and wind through the trees. It upswings around hairpins and glides into new scenes one after another around and through brush and then out into open spaces where we can see canyons stretch away below.

"Beautiful!" I holler to Chris.

"You don't need to shout," he says.

"Oh," I say, and laugh. When the helmets are off you can talk in a conversational voice. After all these days!

"Well, it's beautiful, anyway," I say.

More trees and shrubs and groves. It's getting warmer. Chris hangs on to my shoulders now and I turn a little and see that he stands up on the foot pegs.

"That's a little dangerous," I say.

"No, it isn't. I can tell."

He probably can. "Be careful anyway," I say.

After a while when we cut sharp into a hairpin under some overhanging trees he says, "Oh," and then later on, "Ah," and then, "Wow." Some of these branches over the road are hanging so low they're going to conk him on the head if he isn't careful.

"What's the matter?" I ask.

"It's so different."

"What?"

"Everything. I never could see over your shoulders before."

The sunlight makes strange and beautiful designs through the tree branches on the road. It flits light and dark into my eyes. We swing into a curve and then up into the open sunlight.

That's true. I never realized it. All this time he's been staring into my back. "What do you see?" I ask.

"It's all different."

We head into a grove again, and he says, "Don't you get scared?"

"No, you get used to it."

After a while he says, "Can I have a motorcycle when I get old enough?"

"If you take care of it."

"What do you have to do?"

"Lots of things. You've been watching me."

"Will you show me all of them?"

"Sure."

"Is it hard?"

"Not if you have the right attitudes. It's having the right attitudes that's hard."

"Oh."

After a while I see he is sitting down again. Then he says, "Dad?"

"What?"

"Will I have the right attitudes?"

"I think so," I say. "I don't think that will be any problem at all."

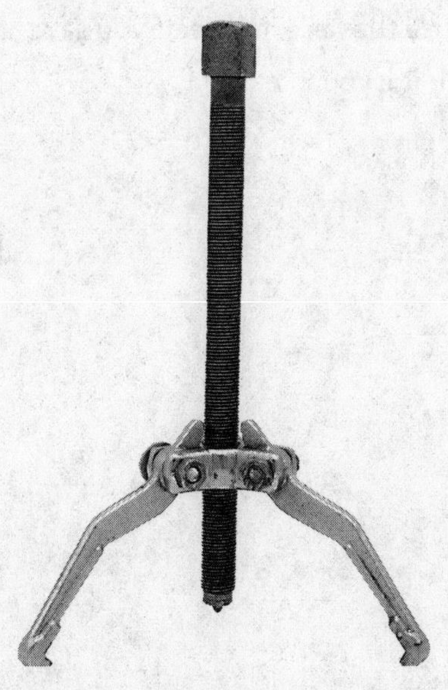

LETTER, MAY 8, 1993

In a subject-object explanation of things, quality is objective and love is subjective. What you love, you say has quality. What you say has quality, you love. In the Metaphysics of Quality, the two are not in separate compartments. They are the same thing. You can call the Metaphysics of Quality the "Metaphysics of Love" and it will be exactly the same, and since Quality and God and Love are considered to be the source of all things there is no problem with E. M. Forster. But you are likely to have difficulties with scientists when you tell them that hydrogen and oxygen combine with each other because they are in love. If you say they *value* the combination it is much easier.

ZEN AND THE ART OF MOTORCYCLE MAINTENANCE: AN INQUIRY INTO VALUES, 1974

There has been a haze, a backup problem in this Chautauqua so far; I talked about caring the first day and then realized I couldn't say anything meaningful about caring until its inverse side, Quality, is understood. I think it's important now to tie care to Quality by pointing out that care and Quality are internal and external aspects of the same thing. A person who sees Quality and feels it as he works is a person who cares. A person who cares about what he sees and does is a person who's bound to have some characteristics of Quality.

Thus, if the problem of technological hopelessness is caused by absence of care, both by technologists and anti-technologists; and if care and Quality are external and internal aspects of the same thing, then it follows logically that what really causes technological hopelessness is absence of the perception of Quality in technology by both technologists and anti-technologists. Phædrus' mad pursuit of the rational, analytic and therefore technological meaning of the word "Quality" was really a pursuit of the answer to the whole problem of technological hopelessness. So it seems to me, anyway.

So I backed up and shifted to the classic-romantic split that I think underlies the whole humanist-technological problem. But that too required a backup into the meaning of Quality.

But to understand the meaning of Quality in classic terms required a backup into metaphysics and its relationship to everyday life. To do that required still another backup into the huge area that relates both metaphysics and everyday life—namely, formal reason. So I proceeded with formal reason up into metaphysics and then into Quality and then from Quality back down into metaphysics and science.

Now we go still further down from science into technology, and I do believe that at last we are where I wanted to be in the first place.

But now we have with us some concepts that greatly alter the whole understanding of things. Quality is the Buddha. Quality is scientific reality. Quality is the goal of Art. It remains to work these concepts into a practical, down-to-earth context, and for this there is nothing more practical or down-to-earth than what I have been talking about all along—the repair of an old motorcycle.

LETTER, MARCH 6, 1993

When an object has quality you love it; when it doesn't you don't. There are different kinds of love: biological, social, intellectual, and Dynamic.

ZEN AND THE ART OF MOTORCYCLE MAINTENANCE: AN INQUIRY INTO VALUES, 1974

The difference between a good mechanic and a bad one, like the difference between a good mathematician and a bad one, is precisely this ability to select the good facts from the bad ones on the basis of quality. He has to care! This is an ability about which formal traditional scientific method has nothing to say. It's long past time to take a closer look at this qualitative preselection of facts which has seemed so scrupulously ignored by those who make so much of these facts after they are "observed." I think that it will be found that a formal acknowledgment of the role of Quality in the scientific process doesn't destroy the empirical vision at all. It expands it, strengthens it and brings it far closer to actual scientific practice.

LETTER, NOVEMBER 20, 1992

The term "love" sometimes refers to a biological emotion, but at other times it refers to a dissolution of the separation between subject and object. In this second instance love seems identical to the perception of Quality.

ZEN AND THE ART OF MOTORCYCLE MAINTENANCE: AN INQUIRY INTO VALUES, 1974

Zen Buddhists talk about "just sitting," a meditative practice in which the idea of a duality of self and object does not dominate one's consciousness. What I'm talking about here in motorcycle maintenance is "just fixing," in which the idea of a duality of self and object doesn't dominate one's consciousness. When one isn't dominated by feelings of separateness from what he's working on, then one can be said to "care" about what he's doing. That is what caring really is, a feeling of identification with what one's doing. When one has this feeling then he also sees the inverse side of caring, Quality itself. . . .

Zen has something to say about boredom. Its main practice of "just sitting" has got to be the world's most boring activity—unless it's that Hindu practice of being buried alive. You don't do anything much; not move, not think, not care. What could be more boring? Yet in the center of all this boredom is the very thing Zen Buddhism seeks to teach. What is it? What is it at the very center of boredom that you're not seeing?

INTERVIEW, 1994, UNIVERSITY OF OSLO

The term "love" is primarily a subjective term, something that exists inside of ourselves. "Quality," on the other hand, has primarily been used in connection with objects that are outside of ourselves. An object has quality, but we have love. The Metaphysics of Quality transcends the subject/object dualism. Whatever we love has quality, whatever has quality we love. They always go together. If you should seriously use the term "love" in science, you would say that hydrogen and oxygen combine because they love each other! The Metaphysics of Quality is really a metaphysics of love.

ZEN AND THE ART OF MOTORCYCLE MAINTENANCE: AN INQUIRY INTO VALUES, 1974

I care about these moldy old riding gloves. I smile at them flying through the breeze beside me because they have been there for so many years and are so old and so tired and so rotten there is something kind of humorous about them. They have become filled with oil and sweat and dirt and spattered bugs and now when I set them down on a table, even when they are not cold, they won't stay flat. They've got a memory of their own. They cost only three dollars and have been re-stitched so many times it is getting impossible to repair them, yet I take a lot of time and pains to do it anyway because I can't imagine any new pair taking their place. That is impractical, but practicality isn't the whole thing with gloves or with anything else.

The machine itself receives some of the same feelings. With over 27,000 on it it's getting to be something of a high-miler, an old-timer, although there are plenty of older ones running. But over the miles, and I think most cyclists will agree with this, you pick up certain feelings about an individual machine that are unique for that one individual machine and no other. A friend who owns a cycle of the same make, model and even same year brought it over for repair, and when I test rode it afterward it was hard to believe it had come from the same factory years ago. You could see that long ago it had settled into its own kind of feel and ride and sound, completely different from mine. No worse, but different.

I suppose you could call that a personality. Each

machine has its own unique personality which probably could be defined as the intuitive sum total of everything you know and feel about it. This personality constantly changes, usually for the worse, but sometimes surprisingly for the better, and it is this personality that is the real object of motorcycle maintenance. The new ones start out as good-looking strangers and, depending on how they are treated, degenerate rapidly into bad-acting grouches or even cripples, or else turn into healthy, good-natured, long-lasting friends. This one, despite the murderous treatment it got at the hands of those alleged mechanics, seems to have recovered and has been requiring fewer and fewer repairs as time goes on.

LETTER, FEBRUARY 1, 1994

In a subject-object metaphysics, "love" and "quality" are separate. Love is subjective, quality is objective. In the Metaphysics of Quality the primacy of the subject/object metaphysical division is dissolved, so that at the highest level of understanding love and Quality are the same thing.

LETTER, FEBRUARY 9, 1994

The Metaphysics of Quality can just as easily be called the "Metaphysics of Love." If you substitute the word "love" wherever you see the word "quality," it will come out the same.

LETTER, JULY 23, 1992

I think that "love" is normally considered to be subjective, and "Quality" is considered [to] be objective. Any object you love has quality. The Metaphysics of Quality denies the dominance of this subject-object metaphysics over Quality, and thus denies it over love too. Love is not subjective. This is exactly what the Christian mystics say.

Quality-love is both undefinable and infinitely definable. It doesn't need a definition, but it can have as many as you want.

LECTURE, 1975, MINNESOTA ZEN MEDITATION CENTER, MINNEAPOLIS

In 1952 I'd been in India for a year and a half. I'd studied at Banaras Hindu University. . . . It was very hot when I got there. . . . I was extremely depressed. It took about a month to overcome the culture shock, I guess you'd call it. I knew it was going to be different, but somehow I expected something better or something more to happen when I hit it. I went to my classes there, and I listened very hard, but I couldn't remember a thing they said. It was in one ear and out the other. The language of Indian philosophy is just an endless proliferation of mountains and mountains of words. They all had a meaning, they were all structured, but it wasn't something I could absorb. . . . And so I was only there for a very short time and I was getting very listless. I started to lose weight. I was down to about ninety-eight pounds at one time. I was in danger of getting very sick, which you knew was very dangerous to be. [There are] very serious diseases there. So I started to wander away in the city to various places and become kind of lost. I felt very guilty about this. I should be studying. I was there on the G.I. Bill. I was supposed to be there memorizing things. But I just kind of wandered through the city, and, looking back on it now, I think I did the best thing I possibly could, because I started to learn in a rather different way. Instead of trying to change things objectively, I'd given up on it. . . .

I'd walk all day in a weakened condition and sometimes sit for long periods of time and brood about things. There was a spot I used to be at day after day . . . just watching the river, staring, gradually performing something unconsciously that was very close to meditation. . . . I was just stopped. I had nothing but despair all around me and so I just sat and watched.

People seemed to sense that; they were very kind to me. There were very few days when someone wouldn't come up and say, "Hi, I see you're in a daze," or something. They would talk to me, invite me to their homes, and I became very enamored with these people. And I learned a lot about India that I couldn't have found out anywhere in the textbook.

EDITOR'S ACKNOWLEDGMENTS

Wendy Pirsig would like to thank the many readers of *Zen and the Art of Motorcycle Maintenance* and *Lila* who corresponded with Robert Pirsig over the years and discussed his ideas in other forums. He was deeply grateful for their engagement throughout his life.

She thanks Lynn Nesbit for suggesting, many years ago, that a volume of best selections of his work might be compiled.

For the publishing of *On Quality*, Wendy is immeasurably grateful that Peter Hubbard picked up on the concept of this book. He has been a wonderful editor to work with, and it was his idea to use the tool photos. She also thanks Molly Gendell, assistant editor, and Liate Stehlik, President and Publisher, Morrow Group.

CREDITS

Some of the material has been previously published in another format.

INDEX

INDEX

ABOUT THE AUTHOR

ROBERT M. PIRSIG (1928–2017) is the author of *Zen and the Art of Motorcycle Maintenance*, which has sold more than five million copies since its publication in 1974, and *Lila*, a finalist for the 1992 Pulitzer Prize for Fiction. He graduated from the University of Minnesota (BA, 1950; MA, 1958) and also attended Banaras Hindu University in India, where he studied Eastern philosophy, and the University of Chicago, where he pursued a PhD in philosophy. Pirsig's papers have been acquired by Harvard University and his motorcycle resides in the Smithsonian Institution. Other Pirsig papers and tools are in the Montana State University archives and Museum of the Rockies, respectively.

ABOUT THE EDITOR

WENDY K. PIRSIG is an archivist who lives in New England. She was married to Robert M. Pirsig from 1978 until his passing.

FORGED IN U.S.A.-V-44504

ABOUT
MARINER BOOKS

Mariner Books traces its beginnings to 1832 when William Ticknor cofounded the Old Corner Bookstore in Boston, from which he would run the legendary firm Ticknor and Fields, publisher of Ralph Waldo Emerson, Harriet Beecher Stowe, Nathaniel Hawthorne, and Henry David Thoreau. Following Ticknor's death, Henry Oscar Houghton acquired Ticknor and Fields and, in 1880, formed Houghton Mifflin, which later merged with venerable Harcourt Publishing to form Houghton Mifflin Harcourt. HarperCollins purchased HMH's trade publishing business in 2021 and reestablished their storied lists and editorial team under the name Mariner Books.

Uniting the legacies of Houghton Mifflin, Harcourt Brace, and Ticknor and Fields, Mariner Books continues one of the great traditions in American bookselling. Our imprints have introduced an incomparable roster of enduring classics, including Hawthorne's *The Scarlet Letter*, Thoreau's *Walden*, Willa Cather's *O Pioneers!*, Virginia Woolf's *To the Lighthouse*, W.E.B. Du Bois's *Black Reconstruction*, J.R.R. Tolkien's *The Lord of the Rings*, Carson McCullers's *The Heart Is a Lonely Hunter*, Ann Petry's *The Narrows*, George Orwell's *Animal Farm* and *Nineteen Eighty-Four*, Rachel Carson's *Silent Spring*, Margaret Walker's *Jubilee*, Italo Calvino's *Invisible Cities*, Alice Walker's *The Color Purple*, Margaret Atwood's *The Handmaid's Tale*, Tim O'Brien's *The Things They Carried*, Philip Roth's *The Plot Against America*, Jhumpa Lahiri's *Interpreter of Maladies*, and many others. Today Mariner Books remains proudly committed to the craft of fine publishing established nearly two centuries ago at the Old Corner Bookstore.

MORE CLASSIC WORKS BY

ROBERT M. PIRSIG

On Quality

"The ultimate goal in the pursuit of excellence is enlightenment."
—Robert M. Pirsig, 1962

For the first time, readers will be granted access to five decades of Pirsig's personal writings in this posthumous collection that illuminates the evolution of his thinking to an unprecedented degree. Skillfully edited and introduced by Wendy K. Pirsig, Robert's wife of four decades, the collection includes previously unpublished texts, speeches, letters, interviews, and private notes, as well as key excerpts from *Zen and the Art of Motorcycle Maintenance* and his second book, *Lila*.

Zen and the Art of Motorcycle Maintenance

50th anniversary edition

With a new foreword by Matthew B. Crawford, bestselling author of *Shop Class as Soulcraft*

The bestselling, highly influential masterpiece about one man's search for meaning on a motorcycle trip through the American West is an enduring roadmap for living a richer, more purposeful existence.

DISCOVER GREAT AUTHORS, EXCLUSIVE OFFERS, AND MORE AT HC.COM.